I0141907

Praise for *"The Way of the Martial Artist!"*

"…read it, and incorporate the lessons and information into your training today. It is a worthy book for any martial artist to read, and I think if you incorporate everything Brett mentions in this book into your own training and life, you can't help but be a better martial artist and lead a more successful positive life."

Alain Burresse
Martial Artist, Author of **Hard-Won Wisdom**
From the School of Hard Knocks and the DVDs:
Hapkido Hoshinsul, **Streetfighting Essentials**, **Hapkido Cane**, the
Lock On Joint Locking Essentials series
www.Burresse.com

"…a comprehensive framework of the numerous principles and concepts you will need to become the best martial artist that you can be."

Shawn Kovacich
Martial Artist, Two-Time World Record Holder
as certified by the Guinness Book of World Records
Author of the **Achieving Kicking Excellence** series
www.Chikara-Kan.com

"Kevin Brett is one of those rare individuals who truly 'gets it,' articulating a framework that can help the newest beginner or the most experienced practitioner make the most of their martial journey, learning not only how to succeed in acquiring warrior skills and mindset, but also how to become successful in all aspects of their lives. … Kevin Brett has written an informative, interesting and useful book that I wholeheartedly recommend."

Lawrence Kane
Martial Artist, Author of **Surviving Armed Assaults** and
Martial Arts Instruction; co-author of **The Way of Kata**,
The Way to Black Belt, and **The Little Black Book of Violence**

The Way of the Martial Artist

"The Way of the Martial Artist is part success manual, part martial arts guide and part survival guide, and all essential!"

Richard Hefner
Martial Artist

"Think of The Way of the Martial Artist as a treasure chest of golden nuggets, each one valuable by itself, but together add up to a mother lode. ... he has miraculously accomplished three things: he covers just enough to tweak the interest of the reader to investigate a subject further; he informs the uninformed that the subject exists and that it's critical to martial arts excellence; and he tweaks the memory of those who know about them but might have grown rusty on certain aspects or have forgotten about them entirely. ... As a guy who has been training, teaching and writing about the martial arts since 1965, I found a wealth of information in this book that I had either forgotten about, had never considered in the first place or had only a partial understanding of, and want to explore further."

Loren Christensen
Martial Artist, Author of more than
40 books, 25 of them on martial arts and numerous DVDs
www.LWCBooks.com

"I remember when I first started training in a traditional martial art, Shotokan Karate, and I went to the book store to find literature on the martial arts. There was not a lot out there except for books on techniques. This is the book that I was looking for at that time, and is a wonderful summary of the different aspects of the martial arts."

Bohdi Sanders, Ph.D.
Martial Artist, Author of **Warrior Wisdom: Ageless Wisdom
for the Modern Warrior** and
Warrior Wisdom: The Heart and Soul of Bushido
www.TheWisdomWarrior.com

The Way of the Martial Artist

Achieving Success in Martial Arts and in Life!

Kevin L. Brett

Kevin Brett Studios, Incorporated

Stafford, Virginia

2008

The Way of the Martial Artist

This book includes information from many sources and gathered from many personal experiences. It is published for general reference and is not intended to be a substitute for qualified martial arts instruction or expert instruction and advice in wilderness survival, or medical advice. This book is sold with the understanding that neither the author nor the publisher is engaged in rendering legal, psychological, medical or other advice related to the topics referenced in this book. The publisher and author disclaim any personal liability, directly or indirectly, for advice or information presented within. Although the author and publisher have prepared this manuscript with utmost care and diligence and have made every effort to ensure the accuracy and completeness of the information contained within, we assume no responsibility for errors, inaccuracies omissions or inconsistencies.

Publisher's Cataloging-In-Publication Data
(Prepared by The Donohue Group, Inc.)

Brett, Kevin L.
   The way of the martial artist : achieving success in martial arts and in life! / Kevin L. Brett.

      p. : ill. ; cm.

   Includes index.
   ISBN-13: 978-0-9819350-0-3
   ISBN-10: 0-9819350-0-1

1. Martial arts--Psychological aspects. 2. Martial arts. 3. Self-realization. 4. Mind and body. I. Title.

GV1102.7.P75 B74 2008
796.8   2008909902

ATTN: Quantity discounts are available to your company educational institution, government agency or martial arts organization.

For more information, please contact the author at Kevin Brett Studios, Inc.
19 Live Oak Lane, Stafford, Virginia 22554 540-845-4755
sales@KevinBrettStudios.com

Dedication

This book is dedicated to my family: my wife Lana Kaye, my son William Alfred and my daughters Alexandra Kaye and Samantha Lee, so that you may develop and maintain strength and confidence and always have the skill and character to summon your warrior spirit should anyone cross your "line of conviction." May you always know the right course and the appropriate response. Always remember that life is about living in the reality of today while reaching for the dreams you have for tomorrow.

Warning & Disclaimer

Marital arts can be lethal and the practice of martial arts or application of various martial arts techniques, training drills and exercises can cause serious injury or death. This book is intended for informational and entertainment purposes. It is not intended as a substitute for a specific martial arts training program by a qualified martial arts school or instructor. You should consult a qualified physician before engaging in any exercise program or physical activities to ascertain whether you or the other participants are mentally and physically healthy enough to engage in such activities.

Martial arts are for defensive purposes only and should be used only as a last resort and only with the least amount of force or technique necessary to reduce the immediate threat or risk in a self-defense situation. Anyone applying fighting or martial arts techniques or methods could be liable in civil or criminal court. You must control your actions and remain within the boundaries of the laws of the jurisdiction in which any defensive techniques may be employed.

The author, publisher and sellers of this book assume no liability for personal injury or damage to property as a result of practicing any concepts or content represented or implied within this book. All individuals are responsible for their own actions. The author, publisher and sellers of this book also provide no warranty or guarantee, expressed or implied that the techniques, concepts or content presented in this book will be effective in any or all self-defense situations.

Contents

Foreword

As I started reading Kevin Brett's, *The Way of the Martial Artist: Achieving Success in Martial Arts and in Life*, the first thing that jumped into my mind was the word, KISS. No, not the awesome heavy metal band that originated in the early 70's with co-founders Gene Simmons and Paul Stanley, but the acronym K.I.S.S. (Keep It Simple Stupid), or as it is also referred to; Keep It Short & Sweet.

Now I know you are asking yourself, "What does K.I.S.S. have to do with this book?" Well that is quite an easy question to answer as the entire premise of this book is to "Keep **It** Short & Sweet." **It** refers to each one of the dozens upon dozens of various principles and concepts that the author discusses in relationship to how they can directly improve various facets of your martial arts skills, which in turn can also indirectly (and in some cases directly) improve various facets of your normal day-to-day life.

Kevin states in the preface of his book, "I do not know all that I would like to about the topics in this book, simply that they require further study by all of us." What exactly does he mean by that? Well, simply put, Kevin takes every principle and concept needed in order to become a proficient and skilled martial artist and explains, in very simple terms, why each one of them is so important to your martial arts training. Any of these many valuable topics is worthy of a book unto itself, but Kevin encourages you to use this book as a roadmap and a guide to seek out those resources which will give you all of the information that you may require on each individual topic.

What makes this book worth reading and ultimately keeping you ask? Well, the answer is quite simply… simplicity itself. This book does not teach you how to punch, kick, block, throw, or any other of the multitudes of actual physical techniques you will find in the various martial arts. Instead, Kevin provides you with a comprehensive framework of the numerous principles and concepts that you will need to understand in order to become the best martial artist that you can be. Use this book to guide your further research on the various principles and concepts that he discusses. Then combine that research with intense study and training in order to obtain the benefits discussed in this book. If you do so, over time you will see a dramatic improvement not only in your ability as a martial artist, but also in your character as a human being.

In the well over twenty-five years that I have been involved in the martial arts, I have literally had several hundred different martial arts books pass through my hands. Of those hundreds of books, most landed on the garbage heap. Some were studied for a time and then sold, and a precious few rated a permanent place in my personal library. Along with those titles that I currently have in my library, I now add Kevin Brett's, *The Way of the Martial Artist: Achieving Success in Martial Arts and in Life!*

Shawn Kovacich
Martial Artist, Two-Time World Record Holder as certified by the Guinness Book of World Records

Author of the *Achieving Kicking Excellence* series

www.Chikara-Kan.com

Preface

This book is for anyone who has a desire to achieve excellence in the pursuit a dream or some lofty goal. The techniques, qualities and methods in this book will help you frame out the elements of your vision and understand the personal qualities and character needed to achieve it. Even if you are not a martial artist, you can still learn and develop the qualities I speak of when I talk about warriors achieving success. The same qualities that help warriors achieve success in their art and in life can help you with any type of challenge or goal. The best part is that if you follow this guidebook to these essential qualities, studies and techniques, you will also find along the way that success is about more than just you. Helping and serving others along the way to achieving your own personal goals reflects a level of self-realization that many overlook in their quest for that often-elusive thing called success.

Martial arts is simply one path toward achieving excellence and this book is a study in what makes a martial artist; what drives one and how that experience equips one to take on new life goals and achieve virtually anything he might set his sights on. My purpose in writing this book is to open doors for you as a fellow martial artist or simply someone who wants to understand better how to develop a black belt mindset.

Many non-martial artists are always fascinated with how we are able to set and achieve a difficult goal such as earning black belt rank. If you are looking to deepen your understanding of martial arts and understand how you can evolve, then this book will give you that. While there are many cookie-cutter martial arts schools willing to take your money and hand you a black belt in twelve to eighteen months along with a seriously false sense of accomplishment and self-confidence, a serious black belt can and should take years to earn. Earning a black belt is a process of maturing in technique, strategy and character. When your maturity and character have reached a higher level, then you may join the ranks of black belts and begin your real studies! Suffice it to say, that journey requires that you have or develop some serious perseverance and make an equally serious commitment to achieve that worthy goal of self-improvement.

So what's the point? The point is that once you have climbed that mountain, you are ready for anything. I will teach you how to understand techniques and training concepts and how to evolve and combine them into effective tactics and strategies. You will learn how to approach an opponent in the ring or an assailant on the street with confidence that the techniques of your style of martial arts will work when strategically applied. Even for non-martial arts endeavors, many of the concepts have great applicability if you take time to consider their utility outside of the study of martial arts.

Most important is how you mature as a person. We often talk about maturity, character, principles and virtues as good things, but do we really know what we're talking about. This book provides those essential insights to help you understand what they are and how to develop them. We all seek a type of inner-peace and harmony in our modern multi-tasking, internet-driven world. We want to feel confident and calm under stress and we wonder if there is more to martial arts and the pursuit of human excellence than simply working up a good sweat. We all wish to realize our potential in many endeavors in our life's journey.

Through martial arts, your potential for human development is unlimited. It is in the endless, shapeless void of self-improvement and enlightenment that the character of a martial artist is shaped and forged through the fires of our will. Begin shapeless; strive to form your own shape; then lose that shape and return to shapelessness. Then you may assume any shape you wish. This is how you will achieve goals. Success is about constantly sculpting and shaping yourself until reality matches your dreams. This book is about the journey between those two points.

Many students spend years wondering when they will feel like they have acquired some greater understanding of this often mysterious and misunderstood art. They wonder when they will feel like they have learned the secrets of the masters. In this book, I have provided insights and perspective for many questions that all martial artists ask who seek to understand the mystery and fascination of human development through martial arts. Maturing as a warrior and an honorable member of society is a noble goal that will take a lifetime and even partial success will enhance your sense of purpose and fulfillment.

Even outside of the pursuit of martial arts, we often struggle to understand human character, emotion and the quest for self-improvement. We all set goals. Some of us succeed. Becoming a black belt is an admirable and challenging mental and physical goal. Much determination and perseverance is required and completing that journey only prepares you to begin the real adventure and set ever-higher goals for yourself!

* * *

The topics I cover are not necessarily bound to particular techniques of punching or kicking. The following pages are concerned with issues that are universal to all styles of martial arts. Beginning students must learn techniques, but they must also begin to exercise their minds and begin to learn, understand and appreciate how to apply techniques, develop strategy and improve their skill levels and their understanding of their art.

Many martial artists are attracted to the physical techniques of the martial arts and never evolve beyond that physical level to gain much insight into effective strategies and honing their cognitive processes. The history, tradition and spiritual aspects of martial arts and the martial psyche captivate many martial artists, but they fail to develop a mastery of the physical and technical aspects of any system. Some martial artists are gifted, balanced and focused enough to develop good skill, good strategy and good spirit.

This book provides practical insights and guidance that martial artists at any level can use to improve in all three essential areas by beginning with understanding key terms and concepts and how they build upon each other. You should not study the specifics of any given style of martial arts to the detriment of understanding how to think about and analyze your progress, development and maturity as a martial artist. This book is a guide to help you progress in the study of your chosen style.

* * *

I have not developed strategies and concepts superior to or even on a par with the great masters. What I have attempted to do is to capture and synthesize some of the insights gained in my own training and those imparted to me by my fellow martial artists. From these I have put together what I consider some of the most important topics of strategy, training and personal development to the student of martial arts who is interested in success. I view these principles as simple truths with universal martial application.

I do not know all that I would like to about the topics in this book, simply that they require further study by all of us. As you begin or continue your training, consider these topics and refine your understanding as you evolve into a martial artist. Keep notes on your progress, discoveries and understanding and in those notes, you will find the seeds of deeper knowledge.

I have tried to keep many of the descriptions high-level so that the student will not get lost in the details. Some of the topics are rather abstract and may require reading more than once and serious reflection. We are all students regardless of rank or years of experience.

Read these passages often and consider them when you train, compete and defend yourself. Some of the passages and thoughts may come across sounding rather Yoda-esque. Hey, it worked for Luke Skywalker! Really, the phraseology is often quite simple, but the concepts are at the core of this art and the pursuit of excellence.

This work is simply my way of expressing what I have perceived to be the essence of martial arts and the spirit of being a martial artist. Train hard and with good spirit, because you are the next generation of martial arts.

The Way of the Martial Artist

Introduction

Life, Liberty and the Pursuit of Happiness

Thomas Jefferson's words echo to us across the centuries. Those words mean something very real to anyone who is serious about realizing a dream or achieving a goal. They are the essential ingredients for success. If you are setting goals, then congratulations; you are alive and you're obviously interested in achieving your potential. You are not content with merely existing. When you set goals and pursue them, you are embodying the essence of Jefferson's words and capitalizing on opportunities to achieve your dreams. Chasing a dream requires that you have freedom and that you exercise your liberty to pursue that dream. Without liberty, your dreams will never materialize. While you are pursuing your passion, you will likely find or make your own happiness. Eleanor Roosevelt said, "The future belongs to those with the courage to chase their dreams."

Pursuing your dreams is a sign of maturity because you are taking personal responsibility and acknowledging that you are solely responsible for your own happiness. Your happiness is not someone else's responsibility. Happiness is not found in some government-funded program or provided to us as an entitlement. It is found within, through individual effort and it does not always come easily. The pursuit of happiness is the first step toward achieving success. The framers of the Declaration of Independence and the U.S. Constitution believed that we should all be able to have the freedom and opportunity to unlock the potential hidden inside each of us and to pursue our aspirations. Their goal was not to provide any of us with what makes us happy. To do so would be an insult to the human spirit. To pursue happiness requires that we have an environment where we are free to find or make our own happiness. That is the path to individual prosperity and that is the legacy and the quest the framers left us.

Chasing a dream and working to achieve a goal is a very liberating experience as you free yourself from the doubt about whether you have the mettle to accomplish something meaningful or remarkable. If you do not have goals and dreams, you are not really living. Pursuing your dream will eventually set you apart from the crowd as you close in on your goals. That is the road to success.

Martial arts is about reaching your potential and achieving personal success. In the course of pursuing a black belt or mastery of a martial arts style, you are beginning to develop personal qualities that can help you achieve goals and success in virtually any area of your life. You will learn to identify and set short-term and long-term goals and develop character qualities that will transform you for life.

One in Ten-Thousand

I am one in ten-thousand. That's right, approximately one of every one hundred people who sign up for a martial arts program make it to first-degree black belt. That's one-percent. Of that one-percent, about one in one hundred ever make it to second-degree black belt. Do the math. One-percent of one-percent is one in ten-thousand or 0.0001 percent. The fact that I was one of five founders of a successful martial arts school puts me in an even higher percentile like one in a million.

That's a level of success that only a few people achieve in martial arts. Ironically, one of my early martial arts instructors told me when I was a blue belt that he didn't think I had what it took to become a black belt. Thanks for the encouragement! Guess I proved him wrong. With that kind of encouragement, who needs detractors?

Am I the greatest martial artist ever? No. I am not on a par with martial arts superstars like Jackie Chan, Bruce Lee or Chuck Norris, but I have achieved a level of success doing something I love that many people struggle to reach if only because they lack the tools, strategy and mindset to do so. And I'm not done yet!

Setting goals and achieving them is critical if you intend to be successful in anything. And let's face it, achieving goals makes life more meaningful and rewarding. At United Karate, we helped many students achieve black belt rank and trained them to be excellent martial artists. We not only taught them the physical techniques however, we emphasized development of their intellect, their character and leadership essentials. With their newly developed skills and character traits, many of our students translated these qualities into every aspect of their life; school, work, relationships, personal and professional goals and many of them were excited to share their achievements with us.

Success is ultimately, what this book is about; achieving your goals in martial arts and in life. Success begins with finding and following your passion. Doing what you love and pursuing your passion in a way that somehow helps other people is always the best way to achieve success. By success, I don't mean that you have executed the perfect formula to develop fabulous wealth and riches; although that could be a beneficial outcome. I mean that you have dreams that involve changing your life or the lives of others. Success begins with a desire to accomplish meaningful goals that help you grow as an individual or to help other people in some capacity. Success comes in many flavors, but they each start with a dream; the unwavering and deep desire needed to power that dream and the commitment to drive the self-discipline that is necessary to convert that dream into reality.

In the world of martial arts, merely achieving black belt rank is not the whole story. There is much more to success than that, but it's certainly a great start and achieving goals like earning a black belt, a college degree, or losing a large amount of weight demonstrates that you have many of the qualities necessary to set goals and achieve them. Earning a black belt can certainly help you develop great habits of success and help you reprogram your mindset and attitude so that moving forward after black belt you will know that anything is possible.

So let's talk success. I was one of the co-founders of the United Karate Institute of Self-Defense, Inc. in Alexandria, Virginia. Three other instructors, my wife (also a black belt) and I decided that we had met way too many highly ranked black belts who had earned numerous trophies in sport karate competition. Sounds great doesn't it. Except for one small problem, virtually every one of these black belt "champions" did not possess even the most basic skills to defend themselves against even a single assailant, much less multiple assailants. What's up with that?

They're black belts. They should be able to leap over tall buildings, outrun bullets, stop a speeding train and run between the raindrops! Right? No, but it certainly seems to the average person that a black belt must be nearly indestructible and probably possesses some almost mystical power and knowledge. Wrong again. If you are not trained properly with a real emphasis on self-defense and street application of martial arts techniques and if you have not developed a survival mindset where your are prepared to respond with lethal force if necessary, then you are merely mimicking movements from your instructor.

Black belts are just ordinary people, but with extraordinary commitment and that's what sets them apart. You will never achieve success in anything until you are committed to it. I can't tell you how many people walked through United Karate's doors and expressed great interest in martial arts. They would not think twice about spending a lot of time describing their fascination and admiration of martial arts and those who study them. That is where their involvement in martial arts ended. They stopped in essentially to tell us that they were interested admirers.

Other visitors simply walked in and said, "Where do I sign?" So what's the difference? Simple, one was interested and the other was committed. Now do you see? Our society is full of dreamers and doers, and a rare, lucky few are blessed to have both qualities. Dreaming and doing ultimately lead to success; whether it's earning your black belt, climbing the corporate ladder (or building your own corporate ladder!) or achieving some other meaningful and challenging personal goal.

That being said, if you have already categorized yourself as either a dreamer or a doer, don't let that deter you from your goals. Just because you tend to have qualities that put you into the dreamer category and have difficulty actually "doing" the things you dream about doesn't mean that you can't realize your dreams. And the same is true for the doers. You must have equal amounts of both and if you do not, then you must strengthen the area in which you are weaker. Wax-on; wax-off. Once you find your passion and pursue something you truly enjoy as we did at United Karate, and you are able to provide a service or value that helps other people, then you can say you are beginning to experience success and achieving your dreams.

Speaking of dreamers, Walt Disney was arguably one of the greatest dreamers of the twentieth century. However, he was also a doer and he surrounded himself with excellent doers to help him realize his dreams. Disney developed a process or a methodology that he and his organization used for every undertaking and project. In fact, he coined the term Imagineer; imagine something, engineer it.

This process is still used today and is taught at the Disney Institute. It is broken down into a number of detailed steps. At its highest level the steps are: Dream, Believe, Dare, Do. There you have it. Start with a dream, whatever it is; believe in the dream and your ability to accomplish it; visualize it; dare others and yourself to join in and work with you to accomplish your dream and finally, do your dream; make it happen.

I could end the book here, but obviously there are a few minor, nagging details that are involved that can spell success as you begin your martial arts studies or continue to an advanced level. This book is structured so that it really doesn't matter if you are a novice or advanced student. You don't even have to be involved in martial arts to gain an appreciation and understanding of some concepts and strategies that can help you in your quest to improve yourself. There's an old saying, (notice how no one ever says, "There's a new saying.") "The more you do of what you've done, the more you'll have of what you've got." Translation; it's time for change. If you want to excel in martial arts or in anything and reap the rewards of sweet success you need to institute some positive changes that will set you on a definite course toward that success.

It's About Survival

Martial Arts are about survival. When you study martial arts, you must learn about many qualities of humanity, both positive and negative. Ultimately, at its core, is the need to survive; be it on the streets of New York City, the jungles of Asia, the deserts of the Middle East or even a hostile business climate. To survive combat and harsh environments, you the martial artist must have many skills and have developed many physical and character qualities. Among these are determination, patience, balance, humility, respect, service, and even compassion.

A martial art is a system of self-improvement on many levels, not merely a library of techniques for kicking, punching and throwing. In order to survive, you must improve yourself beyond your current abilities; physical, mental and spiritual. This book will teach you how to excel in these areas.

This book is not limited to or even concerned with a specific style of martial arts and I do not go into depth on specific techniques. It is a guide on how to study martial arts and how to approach them to gain both a broader perspective on this discipline and at the same time bring into clearer focus the underlying details and concepts that often elude even advanced students. However, most importantly it is about achieving excellence and realizing your greater potential. Becoming a black belt or master in some style of martial arts requires a new mindset and an evolution of your character that will take you to new heights in your art and in life.

As in any other discipline, the practitioner must have a good grasp of the concepts and most importantly the terminology. Many practicing martial artists are too focused simply on technique and conditioning without really learning the actual meanings of the terms they throw around. For example, while many might observe a skilled martial artist and say that he or she is really fast, someone with better insight into the meaning of speed of technique might observe that same practitioner and realize that he is not fast, but rather that the person being observed has excellent timing, which creates the illusion of speed.

Therefore, it is up to the student to learn what the difference is between speed and timing and with this new understanding isolate the two qualities in his mind and practice improving his speed as well as his timing. With the understanding and combination of both qualities the student can significantly increase his skill, strategy and knowledge.

A martial artist is concerned with many things in his training and in his life. He must learn all of the proper techniques for a given style of martial arts; he must consider studying other styles and weapons. He must develop powerful technique and good fighting ability and improve upon his character. There are thousands of training methods, drills, offenses and defenses, but what this all boils down to is everything that a martial artist is concerned with is covered at some level within these pages. To become a black belt or a martial artist with a master's mindset you must seek excellence. Mediocrity is not acceptable.

It's Also about Qualities

This book is all about qualities. The qualities needed to achieve excellence in martial arts and in life. The process of becoming an honorable and purposeful martial artist consists of building on your existing good qualities and reducing or eliminating any less desirable qualities. These qualities are physical, mental and spiritual. I do not mean spiritual in the religious sense, but simply in the sense of a person's character and attitude and impact on the world around him or her. These pages describe these qualities and provide some useful insights about how to develop them, how they build on each other and why they are important.

The *Way of the Martial Artist* explains the physical, mental and spiritual milestones all martial artists should pass on their way to becoming a more mature warrior and an excellent human being. However, remember the best warrior is not warlike, but is able to summon the warrior spirit within when it is required. The warrior spirit is not always shown through combat, but also through compassion, tolerance and service. A warrior is a servant to society. A warrior who has learned the secret to achieving personal excellence must serve as an example and inspiration to others and apply these qualities in all endeavors.

If you learn the language, study and practice the concepts you will improve your physical, mental and character traits and finally in the last chapter as you learn about the psychology and mechanics of success you will be equipping yourself with the tools and habits for success in virtually any undertaking!

Chapter **1**

Origins and Traditions

Understanding the Past

"Those who do not learn the lessons of history are doomed to repeat its mistakes."
Herodotus (Roman Historian)

Since the first time that primitive man discovered that he could trip an adversary by sticking out his foot, fighting techniques have evolved, matured and grown into martial arts systems. Throughout its several thousand-year history, knowledge of the martial arts has primarily been transmitted in the oral tradition. At many times in history, martial arts were outlawed in the orient. Consequently, it was not until the twentieth century that many texts on martial arts began to emerge. Since martial arts were illegal to practice during various times in history and in various countries, committing this knowledge to paper was a risky proposition.

Learning technique only does not help a martial artist mature as an artist; it only helps technique mature, not the soul or character. Bruce Lee and Ed Parker have written many outstanding books on

---

innovative technique, training and strategy in the martial arts. Twenty-four hundred years ago the Chinese military strategist Sun Tzu wrote, *The Art of War*, which dealt with general, strategic concepts of conducting warfare. Sun Tzu's strategies are still in use today and are required reading in most military academies and many corporations. Musashi Miyamoto, considered to be the greatest Japanese swordsman ever, wrote *The Book of Five Rings*. His landmark work expounded upon the concepts of strategy in swordsmanship in classical Japan. In his day, this was self-defense.

These volumes on strategy share a common theme. They remove many of the specifics and particulars of actual fighting techniques and step back to give the student a broader perspective. They reflect upon the psychology of warfare and combat and the application of the mind, not merely the might. Many of the principles and concepts are valid and applicable in contexts other than martial arts, open warfare or personal self-defense. These seminal works and many others capture some of the core concepts of martial arts and combat. They are part of the ancient and modern history of the art.

It is difficult to say exactly where martial arts began. Ancient Greeks and Romans practiced various forms of wrestling and grappling. We all know of the Roman gladiators and their skill in the arena. The Zulu warriors, the Spartans, the Samurai, the Hwa Rang, the Shaolin Monks and many other warrior cultures are all part of the vast array of cultures and styles that have contributed to the rich heritage of martial arts.

Many sophisticated martial arts techniques and systems were developed in India several thousand years ago. Kaliripayat is one in particular that is still in practice today. As trade routes and the silk roads opened up from China to India, it was only natural that martial arts techniques and knowledge would find its way along these same routes. Martial systems and fighting styles had been evolving in China for several millennia as well. Monks at the legendary Shaolin temple developed a system known as Shaolin temple boxing. Today, Buddhist monks from one of the oldest

Shaolin temples travel the world and give public exhibitions of their martial skills.

Legend has it that an Indian monk named Bodhidharma (more commonly Da Mo) left India and arrived some time later at the Shaolin temple in China. There is debate among historians as to whether there was only a single Shaolin temple or several scattered across China. Nonetheless, he arrived at one of the temples and began to impart his knowledge to the very receptive monks.

Da Mo taught fighting techniques to the Shaolin monks. He taught them deep breathing techniques and many concepts related to what we know today as Yoga. He also emphasized the importance of training the mind in meditation. Legend also states that at one point, he spent nine years meditating in a cave sitting facing the wall of the cave watching ants and listening to them scream. As a demonstration of respect, one Shaolin monk cut off his hand and gave it to Da Mo.

Bodhidharma

The introduction of Indian fighting techniques was a catalyst that spawned a golden age in Chinese martial arts. Innovation and experimentation in Chinese systems helped to continue to evolve the various styles and systems.

Monks began to study nature and its effects on the environment for inspiration. They sought a model from which they might derive useful concepts upon which to base martial techniques and systems. Chinese monks studied the effects of wind, rain, fire and water on earth. These were the essential elements and they became known as the five elements. Techniques were categorized according to the elements to which they corresponded. Techniques could be labeled water techniques if they were soft and supple or if they were hard and crashing. An example of water techniques can be found in the Korean Tae Kwon Do variant of Chung Do Kwan meaning Blue Wave School.

Monks also looked to animals and insects. They studied their fighting techniques and survival behaviors to extract useful knowledge. Many Chinese systems arose around techniques that were based on animal movement. Examples that are still taught today include, Tiger Claw Kung Fu, Drunken Monkey Kung Fu, Crane and Eagle Claw Kung Fu.

Kung Fu deep back stance

In China, around 300 B.C, Lao Tzu an ascetic and sage was the first to write down the philosophy of Taoism; the way. Taoism is an ancient Chinese philosophy based upon three core concepts: humility, compassion and moderation. Taoists practice wu wei, the principle of non-action, naturalness. They strive to achieve simplicity or emptiness. Taoists recognize and believe that there is a strong relationship that people have to nature, which leads to greater understanding and enlightenment.

Tzu was a recluse who spent most of his life in nature. Many soft martial arts of China including T'ai Chi are based on his teachings and observations of nature. He recorded these teachings and analysis in his timeless work the *Tao Te Ching;* the book of changes.

The weakest things in the world can overmatch the strongest things in the world.

Nothing in the world can be compared to water for its weak and yielding nature; yet in attacking the hard and the strong nothing proves better than it, for there is no alternative to it.

The weak can overcome the strong and the yielding can overcome the hard; this all the world knows but does not practice.

-    *Lao Tzu*

The Eight Tri-grams of the Pa-Kua

Names and symbolism of the Pa-Kua

Name	Attribute	Image
Creative	Strong	Heaven
Gentle	Penetrating	Wind, Wood
Arousing	Inciting, Movement	Thunder
Abysmal	Dangerous	Water
Still	Resting	Mountain
Receptive	Devoted, Yielding	Earth
Clinging	Light-giving	Fire
Joyous	Joyful	Lake

The table above shows the names, meanings and symbolism of the tri-grams. Many martial arts styles, techniques and philosophies were based on interpretation and application of these concepts and the Pa-Kua served as a unifying symbol of philosophy, enlightenment and martial styles and concepts.

Confucianism is a related philosophy that asserts that through the training of the mind and embracing the principles of human virtue that you can become a "superior person". Confucianism strives for balance. A central belief is to do the right thing and to have the strength to stand up to people such as tyrants who stand in the way of a better society. A central practice of Confucianism is that you spend time reading and educating yourself, learn the arts, and study individuals who exhibit characteristics that make them true and honorable role models.

Chinese systems often are somewhat of a family affair in nature, meaning that they were often developed by the patriarch of a family and practiced by that family and its descendents. In due time, the Chinese systems, including a vastly rich collection of weapon systems and techniques found its way to the East and South to countries like Japan, Okinawa, Korea, Viet Nam, Cambodia, Burma, Thailand and the Philippines where Chinese based systems blended further with the native systems and fighting arts of those lands.

During much of ancient martial arts history, the martial arts themselves were outlawed at various times. Local warlords who would use trained martial artists in the form of monks from the local temples would then forbid the monks to teach or train others for fear that they would then rise up against the warlord themselves. Because these monks were so highly skilled and their abilities were feared by rival political or military leaders, the penalties and punishments for teaching martial arts were severe and often included execution. It is for this reason that many martial arts system and techniques were often not written down and if they were that knowledge was carefully guarded.

Most martial knowledge was therefore passed on in the oral tradition from instructor or master to student. Often martial arts techniques and systems were disguised to look like exercise, dance or cultural rituals so that they could be practiced without arousing suspicion. Spies would often attend training sessions where martial arts were rumored to be practiced. All except the most senior and trusted students would be taught only symbolic meanings for various movements and not the actual practical self defense application for fear that a spy might be lurking amongst the general population of a training hall where the dance or

---

exercise was being taught. Even in times when it was legal to teach martial arts systems, the true meanings of techniques were usually not taught except to senior instructors because the masters feared their prized knowledge and secret techniques would become common knowledge and thus possible to defeat, hence the shrouded and seemingly mystical nature of martial arts.

Fighting Systems and Martial Arts

Martial arts have a spiritual and ethical foundation and a governing philosophy, fighting systems do not. For example, Krav Maga (a Hebrew term meaning close combat) is the Israeli system of self-defense used by the Israeli military. It is very effective and deadly like many martial arts, but it is a fighting system rather than a martial art. It consists of tactical concepts and techniques, some overall guiding principles for engaging in combat and nothing more. It is highly effective, but it has no philosophical component or spiritual aspect to it.

A martial art may contain philosophical elements that train an artist to avoid confrontation or mitigate risk. It will prepare you to consider carefully the fact that you are about to cause serious or even fatal consequences to an aggressor who is still another human being. By contrast, a fighting system will simply address the fact that an aggressive act has occurred which requires an appropriate physical response. There is no consideration other than to cause maximum damage to the other individual. More of the key elements of character, spirit and philosophy will be covered later.

Bushido: Ethics for Warriors

A Buddhist monk developed a code of behavior and conduct for the Japanese Samurai warriors. The Samurai were the warrior class in feudal Japan. Their code of conduct was known as Bushido – warrior way. The Bushido was essentially a book of manners that described in detail exactly how a Samurai should act in every situation from daily life to combat and in death. Bushido added a spiritual and philosophical component to the fighting techniques and tactics of the various Japanese martial arts that these warriors studied. It was the next level of evolution and maturity toward true martial arts for the Japanese.

Samurai in Kabuki costume

Certainly, a system of ethics and etiquette like this was not what the creators of Krav Maga had in mind when they were developing

---

techniques and tactics for neutralizing an aggressor. Bushido was a way of life and it dictated Samurai behavior completely. In Krav Maga the assumption is, there are no rules in a fight. They are two opposite ends of the philosophical spectrum.

Samurai became the educated elite class of Japanese society. They were the ruling class. The fact that Samurai were educated or considered the elite or dominant and controlling class in Japan does not suggest that all Samurai were wealthy. Many Samurai were not wealthy and in fact lived in poverty. However, Samurai were, nonetheless, the only members of Japanese society allowed to wear and use the Samurai swords, Katana, Wakazushi and Daito. You could not train to become a Samurai, you must have been born into a Samurai family; the son of a Samurai. And of course in the patriarchal Japanese society, only men could be Samurai. The Samurai class actually had as many as two-hundred and fifty levels or layers. Those fortunate few who were born into the upper level strata of the Samurai class would fare better in life than those born into the lower classes of Samurai. However, even the lowliest Samurai was higher in society than the highest merchant, artisan or peasant farmer.

Warriors and Tea

There is an old Samurai saying that a man who does not have tea in him cannot truly appreciate beauty and truth. Japanese society evolved highly ritualized actions and activities as part of Samurai life. Every movement was carefully choreographed with painstaking attention to detail and consistency. This highly structured approach to even simple activities was intentionally developed to help symbolize the perfect order and harmony possible in such highly structured situations. These rituals and ceremonies also teach and maintain discipline, respect and order.

The preparation and drinking of tea became the tea ceremony. The finer points of the tea ceremony were taught to Samurai so that they might become more refined in their social graces. The ability to concentrate, and have such a simple pleasure and sensory experience be the focus of so much attention, detail and ritual actually was a training method for Samurai to hone their perceptual skills and ultimately their combat skills. What appeared on the surface to be charm school for Samurai was actually mental training for combat.

The tea ceremony was symbolism for what Samurai strived to achieve in Zen meditation and the practice of their martial skills; eat when you are eating, drink when you are drinking, sleep when you are sleeping. The tea ceremony was codified and refined and practiced in its most minute details with the same attention to detail and refinement that martial artists use when practicing their techniques. The Japanese approach toward many things of importance and reverence was to codify the rules, processes and behaviors of key aspects of daily life.

These ceremonies helped to underscore the importance of the event in the lives of Samurai and other citizens. The order brought about by ritualizing and formalizing activities like tea ceremonies emphasized the importance and desirability of order in the universe and in life. Order is good. Structure is good. Disorder and lack of structure is bad.

The shape and form of the Samurai class evolved from the ninth century until its culmination in the nineteenth century. In its last few centuries, the Samurai became the military and governmental elite in Japan. As part of that class, it became required and expected that Samurai were well-educated, possessed social graces, were capable of artistic expression and of course were skilled in martial arts.

Samurai were taught and practiced flower arranging, they learned musical instruments and music composition, they pursued studies in painting, calligraphy and poetry. Why would warriors need to know these things? How do these practices relate to combat and martial arts?

Like many modern military academies, the Japanese wanted and expected their Samurai to be well educated and well rounded in their skill, knowledge and abilities. For Samurai to truly be the elite, they must be on a par with those considered to be the elite in most other societies especially those in the West. The pursuit and practice of these various art forms and activities also helped the Samurai practice focus, concentration and attention to detail. Samurai learned patience and perseverance through a variety of outlets.

By contrast, modern martial systems are not focused on culture and artistic endeavors such as flower arranging and the tea ceremony. A recent addition to the martial world, for example is the United States Marine Corps Martial Arts Program (MCMAP). This innovative system with its slogan of "One Mind, Any Weapon" has a wide variety of specific close quarters combat techniques. MCMAP is indeed a true martial art with both a philosophical and moral/ethical element to it as well as physical conditioning and specific martial techniques and weapons – no flower arranging.

MCMAP also has a system of various belt ranks, and stresses mental and character development, teamwork, leadership, citizenship and the responsible use of force. All Marines are required by the Commandant of the Marine Corps to earn their Tan belt; the first rank. Any Marines deployed in theaters of combat are required to earn their gray belt; the second rank, and all infantry Marines are required to earn their green belt. The program is designed to help the Marines to develop the mind, body and character simultaneously and equally.

The Marines study martial history and culture. They have required reading including the *Art of War* and master a variety of rough terrain skills. Studies examine societies that produce warriors either primarily or exclusively. Examples include the Apache Indians, the Spartans and the Zulus.

These ancient martial styles continue to find new life and new application in modern life and help modern warriors prepare for and fight the conflicts of the twenty-first century by building on the techniques and concepts of several millennia of martial heritage.

U.S. Marines practicing ground fighting in the rain as part of the MCMAP.

Musashi Miyamoto

A martial education would not be complete without some familiarity with this truly legendary figure. Essentially he and Sun Tzu's *Art of War* were the inspiration for this book. One of the most famous Samurai was Musashi Miyamoto. Musashi wrote *The Book of Five Rings*, which described the approach and strategy of studying the sword and combat strategy in general. His book has applicability on many levels and in many disciplines. Today almost every business school and office supply store has copies of this book in the business section. It is timeless and like a truly good book on strategy, always just beyond the complete grasp of the student. His concepts, their application and interpretation are always subject to more discussion, analysis, re-interpretation, and evaluation.

Musashi Miyamoto

There are many stories and legends surrounding Musashi. He favored the bokken, the wooden training sword, over an actual metal blade. Legend states that he defeated at least sixty opponents in mortal combat to prove the superiority of his style of swordsmanship. His most famous legend is the story where a prince in a wealthy Samurai family challenged him. The prince was highly skilled in swordsmanship. The two agreed to meet at a specific time on a nearby island where they would dual to discover the superior swordsman. The prince was punctual. Musashi overslept, and on the boat ride to the island as he allegedly recovered from a hangover. He fashioned a primitive bokken from an oar using a knife. He arrived several hours late to find the prince furious. The two faced off and with one blow, Musashi's bokken felled the prince. Musashi returned to the mainland. He spent the last several years of his life writing his *Book of Five Rings*.

Hwa Rang Warriors

While the Japanese shaped and evolved their elite Samurai warrior class, Korea developed an elite band of highly skilled, highly educated warriors called the Hwa Rang. One of the under belt patterns in the traditional Chon Ji Hyungs (patterns) developed by General Choi, the founder of the International Tae Kwon Do Federation is named for these famous warriors.

The Hwa Rang studied history, the arts and sciences. They were expert in martial arts and were skilled in wilderness survival techniques. They trained for brutal conditions and in extreme types of weather. The Hwa Rang were the "Warriors of Flowering Manhood." They swore loyalty to king and country. Hwa Rang were the Korean equivalent of the Japanese Samurai. Both Hwa Rang and Samurai were Asian counterparts to the European knights who also strived for high levels of conduct, morality and virtue to compliment their warrior training. These are many of the same qualities shared by the ancient Spartans and their warrior culture.

Throughout history and across nearly all continents there have arisen cultures of warriors who have sought to enhance and enlighten their existence and their pursuit of lethal combat skills. In fact the pairing of social graces, artistic expression and moral underpinnings with the most primitive of human behaviors – that of mortal engagement with another being seems almost an intentional, if not conscious effort to tame, balance and counteract these primal almost animalistic behaviors with something seemingly more human certainly on a higher plane of existence.

T'ai Chi Chuan

Many of us have seen people practicing T'ai Chi. We think of it as moving meditation, a graceful exercise for older citizens. Few know that it is a martial art and that each movement has a practical and lethal application in self-defense just as do the kata of the hard-styles. The Chi refers to Chi energy and the ability to control and direct this energy and maintain it. T'ai Chi makes use of the centers of the body; the upper center, the middle center and the lower center. These are the centers of balance, of power, and spirit.

It is useful for you to practice their kata in slow motion as a T'ai Chi practitioner. This way you may discover the subtle movements and aspects of your techniques and improve and focus on their details. T'ai Chi, when applied at normal speed in self-defense is as effective as any style of martial arts in providing self-defense. It is even rumored that Genghis Kahn studied T'ai Chi and understood its combat application.

Unfortunately, many who study T'ai Chi today are not even aware of its rich martial heritage and simply focus on its symbolism and meditative aspects. This is much the way other martial arts are taught in the more commercial settings. The true meaning and combat applications are lost. Regardless of the style or system of martial arts you may be studying, the following chapters provide fundamental concepts, skills, strategies and character development that will help you become a more successful martial artist and person.

Ninjas

Japanese Ninjas are certainly the stuff of legend and the subject of many movies, but the reality is that they were skilled in a wide variety of unconventional weapons and tactics. Ninjas existed for hundreds of years in Japan and were the original Special Forces commandos. Ninjas were masters of disguise, camouflage, concealment, explosives and deception. Ninjas learned and trained in a variety of close combat techniques drawn from various more established Japanese arts. They served as intelligence agents and assassins. With these skills and capabilities, Ninjas have left an indelible mark on history and earned a key place in the history of martial arts. In fact, it could be argued that Ninjas have played a significant role in martial arts history and because of their diversity of techniques and tactics and effectiveness, they have served as the blueprint for all modern Special Forces. Navy SEALs in particular employ a wide variety of weapons, tactics, explosives, concealment, stealth and other skills directly attributable to Ninja operations.

Chapter 2

Skill and Training

Training the Body

"A journey of a thousand miles begins with the first step."
Chinese Proverb

Skills are the basic mechanical abilities and techniques that every martial artist or fighter must have to be effective in combat. They are the physical foundation and the starting point for everyone. Skill develops the body of the martial artist. Any goal or objective you may choose to pursue will almost certainly involve the development and use of some new set of skills.

As a martial artist, you must develop these skills regardless of your particular art. To develop these skills you must understand the terms and concepts. Study these carefully and make these concepts an integral part of your training and workouts. As you practice and study the concepts of this chapter, you will be improving your physical technique and body, but you will be expanding your mind through a more in-depth understanding of the topics.

Adaptability

This is the ability to respond rapidly, effectively and without confusion to changing stimuli. These stimuli can be different training conditions. They can be new techniques, styles of martial arts, weapons or changes in lighting, temperature, speed, distance, surface, or any other attribute of your environment.

To survive, welcome change by varying your training as I have mentioned. The more you do this, the better equipped you are to adapt effectively, because you are always doing it. Many martial arts systems have training sessions where their students practice their martial arts in the rain, snow, mud, swamps and other rough and difficult terrain. In this manner, students learn to be aware of environmental factors, but also filter out distractions and focus on defeating their opponent.

Do not become frustrated as circumstances change or vary. Welcome this. Anything else would be boring. Variety improves and maintains your survival skills. You cannot possibly adapt if you are not first aware of what is around you to which you can learn to adapt! If you can adapt, you may survive and martial arts are about survival.

Adaptability can also refer to using your environment. For example, you may use your environment by grabbing a handful of sand to throw in your opponent's eyes. You may grab a branch lying on the ground to strike your opponent or shove them headfirst into a vertical pole support inside a subway car or city bus. These are examples of using features of the terrain or surrounding environment to your advantage to augment your martial techniques. Typically, these are weapons of opportunity.

Versatility

This is not the same as adaptability. You may be good at adapting, but you may not be very versatile. On the other hand, you may be very versatile, but have difficulty adapting.

Versatility is important to the martial artist because you emphasize a wide variety of techniques and tactics, which give you an edge over someone less versatile.

Versatility is having a broad range of skills; you can kick well, punch well, move well, think well etc. Versatility is the quality of having many skills; adaptability is the ability to acquire new skills readily. As you become more versatile, you will gradually become more adaptable. Do not confuse these two.

Diversity in Training

The mind is a curious thing, it responds favorably to a variety of stimuli, but when it receives the same inputs repeatedly, it becomes bored. When there is no change to the stimuli, these inputs cease to stimulate and the mind seeks other inputs.

What this means to the serious martial artist is that he or she must train in new ways and in new places. Train outside sometimes, inside at other times. Train fast sometimes, slowly at other times. Train with a large group at some times and by yourself with no distractions at other times. Train in silence some times and with noise or music at others. Train in the heat and in the cold.

All of these variations in your training will make it easy for you to stay focused, because your mind will always be alert to the changing stimuli. This is the first step toward learning to become adaptable. Adaptability is crucial to survival.

As you vary your training methods and environment, you are constantly becoming aware of things that you would not have noticed if you trained the same way in the same environment all the time. This awareness of conditions and circumstances is essential in learning to adapt. In nature, those species that learn to adapt to their environment survive. It is the same for martial artists.

Realism

The more realistic the training experience . . . the less shocking reality will seem. Part of varying your training is practicing for realism. Take your training seriously. If it is a joke or becomes too much of a social gathering, you will be easily surprised or overwhelmed in a real situation. As I described earlier, some schools of martial arts practice in swamps, rain, and all types of terrain and environments. Martial arts are a war fighting skill where realism is a key ingredient. Part of the reason for the diversity and variation in training is to introduce different realistic elements. A curious thing happens when you make a training drill very realistic, you become uncomfortable. Reality isn't always pleasant, but reality is what you are training for. Being uncomfortable is a good thing. Get used to it in training so that you will not be surprised if it happens for real.

Coordination

Coordination is a skill you must develop just like many other qualities. You are born with a certain amount of coordination for your particular body. You must work to maintain and improve this. Coordination is the ability to make the body do what the mind requires.

Visualization helps coordination. Picture what you are trying to do. If you cannot picture it, it will be more difficult to accomplish. Therefore, coordination consists of mating the mind's vision with the body's ability. Many different things may affect your level of coordination positively or negatively; timing, speed, balance and flexibility are just a few.

As you practice coordination with different drills, you will see that it becomes easier to adapt. I have already discussed the importance of adaptability in martial arts. As you improve at adapting, you will become more coordinated. The other part of coordination is distance judgment. If you reach too far or not far enough because you have misjudged the distance, then you will need to practice distance improvement. This will aid your coordination.

One of the best ways to improve coordination is simply to drill your various kicks, punches and other technique endlessly. What happens over time is that you body becomes programmed and develops the necessary muscle memory and improved technique so that you move more gracefully and confidently. I have seen many students, particularly adults, come in at the start of the martial arts training. They can barely put one foot in front of the other and walk without tripping on themselves. After a few short months of training in different stances and working through the movements in the kata, they are able move with ease because their muscles had never really been taught to do anything requiring any degree of coordination. They realized that coordination is not something you are born with, but that like balance, it is a skill that must be developed.

Timing

Many people confuse timing and speed. They are not the same. Someone can be fast, but have poor timing. Someone can have excellent timing, but be slow. There is a difference. You will see this when you focus and isolate these two qualities as you train and observe others.

- - - - - - - - - -

In order for timing to work, you must first know your speed. Begin to focus more on how long it takes you to execute a movement. You can gradually improve your speed with drills, but at some point, we all reach our own natural speed limit. Many factors will determine your individual speed limit including age, joint mobility, muscle flexibility; even the speed at which your muscles and tendons react to nerve impulses will affect your speed. To add more complexity, your speed will be different on any given day due to how you feel on that day.

You may be slow, but if you know the speed of your strike, then you can time when to begin your strike so that it will hit its mark. Developing speed is good, because a fast, well-timed technique is much harder to avoid than a slower, well-timed technique.

*Improving your sense of speed and distance will
improve your timing.*

By knowing the speed of all of your techniques you will know how much time you need to strike. If a situation does not allow enough time for a particular strike, then use another, less time-consuming technique. Be conscious of these factors of timing, speed and your own limiting factors will improve your fighting skill and responsiveness.

Distance

Know not just the speed of your techniques, but the distance that they require or can cover. Timing and speed are of no use if distance is unknown. When you know the speed of your technique, the distance and the timing, you can be effective. You must have all of these to have a complete technique. If any of these are unknowns or missing, then the technique cannot work except by luck.

Practice distance-training drills with both stationary and moving targets with kicks and hand techniques. Focus on being able to accurately judge the distance to a given target whether it is moving or fixed. Once you know the distance required for a given strike you can focus on improving speed and reaction time. Distance judgment will help you know how much speed to apply for a given block, strike or kick.

Speed and Reaction

There are many ways to improve reaction time, but there is only one way to practice speed. Practice lightning fast kicks and punches by kicking and punching with lightning fast speed. It is that simple.

To practice speed, make yourself uncomfortable. You will be breathing heavier and you will feel that you have exerted yourself. That is the difference between feeling at ease and moving fast.

To improve your speed you must develop flexibility and strength equally. Flexibility will remove resistance. When your mind knows that your flexibility is limited, it will hold you back from your maximum speed potential. Your joints must also have good range of motion and mobility to promote speed and good reaction time.

When you know that you are quite flexible or that you have significantly improved your muscle flexibility, your mind will have no reservations about your body moving with maximum speed and reach. Improved strength will give you the muscle needed to project or retract as you move with speed in any direction. Improved strength does not always mean larger muscles. Remember, muscle has mass and mass that you must overcome before you can attain speed. The larger you are the longer it will take to achieve any degree of speed.

There is a difference between being able to move fast and having fast reflexes or reactions. Fast reaction means that you can reach high speed in a short amount of time. Those who have more mass to overcome will generally have slower reactions, but even a person with slow reactions can eventually reach high speed. You want both.

Balance

Balance in movement and posture means that you should be able to smoothly, shift weight or adjust muscles that are supporting you and your position. When trying to deceive an opponent you will need to develop the ability to cause this shift in balance invisibly and imperceptibly so that your opponent will not notice and you will have the advantage.

To move, stand, sit, kick or punch in a jerky, awkward way is not to have balance. Real balance means knowing when, where and how much to move to stay in this position without thinking about it. Know what to do without thinking. If you must think about it, you do not have balance, because you cannot think of balance and fight at the same time. If you do not have balance, you cannot fight.

- - - - - - - - - -

Balance exists in many aspects. A good martial artist must have balance between offense and defense, punching and kicking, physical and mental abilities. Only when a martial artist has developed strength in all aspects and has balanced these strengths is he or she a truly good martial artist.

Posture

Posture relates strongly to balance. Be in a stance without being in it. This is not obvious, but it is simple after you have grasped its meaning.

You should naturally assume a defensive or offensive stance or posture. The stance should simply occur as part of your perception of your opponent. When you perceive the need for a certain stance or position, you are already in the stance.

Be at ease and at rest, but be ready to strike or defend. Tension burns energy, tightens muscles and slows down reaction or action because you must first remove the tension before an action or reaction can occur. This affects timing, balance, speed, power, and many other things.

Good martial arts posture is concerned with four things: maintaining balance, making your weapons (arms, legs, hands) available for use, facilitating smooth, balanced and rapid movement from one position or posture to the next and protecting vulnerable targets.

The defender executes a hip throw against her opponent who attacked from the rear.

Movement

Movement, like balance, should not be a thought consciously acted upon to take effect. Movement should be free flowing and constant or as required, not started and stopped as a conscious idea interrupted.

- - - - - - - - - -

If movement begins from a static position, then the beginning of the movement should not be sudden or noticeable. When a movement ends and you assume a static position, this transition should not be obvious or attract much attention. Your opponent should not immediately notice when you began to move or when you completed a movement.

- - - - - - - - - -

Movement should be the same as intention. You should drive your intentions by your perception of your opponent. When you perceive what your opponent is doing, make your movement follow and flow naturally. This all requires a heightened sense of visual and perceptual skill to see, notice, interpret and respond to an opponent. If your intentions and your movement are one in the same, there is no thought or decision to move, you simply move, as you perceive your opponent. This is the essence of reaction. It is subconscious and the mechanics of sight, interpretation, movement and response that you once practiced consciously to isolate and develop individually, now meld into subconscious to form skillful reaction and response.

If you were to first perceive your opponent, then decide upon your intentions, then turn these intentions into movements, it would be too late and your opponent would have gotten the better of you. That is why movement and intentions must be one, driven initially by perception.

Footwork

Do allow yourself to focus much on learning particular foot movements; this will actually restrict your movements like following a particular dance step. You should become familiar with basic stances that are natural and unexaggerated. Stances must be practical and facilitate movement. Stances must facilitate transition from one to another easily. A good stance also makes good balance possible and provides a stable base or platform from which to fight.

Learn to move smoothly, gracefully, with speed, balance and purpose without thinking about your footwork. There are times to be light on your feet. This means being on the balls of your feet, with knees bent as if in a stance, but as before without being in it. During these times, you do not want to be in one place for long or your opponent will have you.

Footwork must contribute to and help you maintain balance and posture. Footwork should never cause balance points to be unsupported except for a fleeting instance when you are moving and adjusting several balance points simultaneously to assume a new stance or posture. There are times to be solid and firmly planted on your feet so that you cannot be moved. You must know which is appropriate, lightness or solidness of the feet.

These stances are not too low or dramatic and it is easy to move the legs and hips from one position to the next: (left to right: back stance, horse-riding stance, front stance). These stances provide superior balance to very low stances.

Breathing

You must learn how to breathe. This is not obvious. Pulling and pushing air to and from the lungs is not breathing. Breath control is essential as a regulator of your energy.

Shallow breathing from the chest is little more than huffing and puffing. Deeper breathing from the lower part of the lungs and the diaphragm is true breathing.

With true breathing, you fare giving your body time to take in the oxygen and put it to full advantage. If you do not breathe deeply through the diaphragm with good, relaxed control, you will quickly tire and your opponent will have you. Breathe from the bottom of your lungs to the top. Most people breathe from the top of their lungs to the bottom. This is incorrect for the martial artist who demands more from his body than others.

You must practice pulling the air in quickly, but letting it out slowly. As you let it out slowly, your lungs are given time to do their work, remove waste and take in the good oxygen. Any other efforts at breathing are meaningless.

I have found an effective method of oxygenating the body during meditation and stretching and during brief rest periods in the middle of a workout. The breathing exercise is an eight-count exercise that you repeat ten times. Take a rapid, deep breath on the first count. Relax your stomach muscles so that the diaphragm may expand and you can pull it downward by the relaxation of your stomach muscles. This allows more air to enter the lungs. Hold the air in your lungs for counts two through six, and then exhale on seven and eight. This forces the air to remain in your lungs long enough to extract more oxygen from each breath. The result is that you quickly oxygenate your body and you become more mentally alert, and physically energized. You can repeat this drill for ten repetitions any number of times during the day whenever you feel that an increased level of oxygen will help improve your performance, alertness or general well-being.

Relaxation

Relaxation is one of the first and most difficult lessons that the martial artist must learn. You cannot really be taught how to relax; it must be discovered and practiced.

- - - - - - - - - -

To be relaxed is to be prepared to perceive. When a martial artist is able to perceive his opponents intentions without a bad attitude or anger or other distractions of the moment, then the martial artist can counter them.

To be in a state other than relaxation such as tension is to be distracted by other things or thoughts and to not be capable of full awareness.

When you are free of tension, ego or negative attitude, you can be aware. If you are aware, then you can perceive your opponent fully. Then your intentions of what to do will flow smoothly, undistracted from your perceptions.

Focus

Focus requires awareness. If you are not aware, you cannot focus. To be aware you must first be relaxed and free of tension. These distractions take away your focus. Practice relaxation. Relaxation frees the mind and body of distractions. When these are gone, then there is room for awareness and focus. There are times to focus on clearing the mind first in order to begin something new and there are times to tune in the mind to something specific and tune out other environmental distractions so that the subject of your focus has your full attention. Both clearing and tuning the mind are skills that require practice. You can achieve these skills purposefully through meditation. As your ability to meditate improves, you will be able focus or change focus more rapidly as needed in a dynamic combat situation. This ability to focus where and when needed, will prepare you to adapt to whatever may come your way.

Meditation

Martial artists borrow tradition from various Asian warrior monks. Monks practice meditation for religious contemplation. Meditation by martial artists is not for religious fulfillment, but for contemplation, focus and channeling of Chi and enlightenment. You can use meditation for several purposes, to solve a problem, to empty the mind, to find an answer, to discover harmony, direction, organization, peace and to embrace the enlightenment. The sun is the light force in our solar system. It emanates its positive energy to the planets and the energy transfers to them and is absorbed; and it gives life. The absence of this light takes life away.

A martial artist meditates to empty the mind and the ego before a training session. He or she must empty the cup of their emotions, thoughts and desires and prepare the mind, body and spirit. You must align the Chi of the body positively to prepare the student or the expert to absorb new knowledge and to reach higher levels of understanding, insight and attainment of skill in the course of your workout.

Meditate and focus on light. Focus on a conscious awareness of your thoughts. What are the positive thoughts and what are your negative thoughts? Focus on the positive thoughts. Replace negative perspectives and energy with positive. Change your thoughts from negative to positive. This is preparation for experiencing a more effective, productive and positive training session. This is a preparation for a more positive outcome to relationships and events in your life.

Change your thoughts and you will change your actions, your outcomes and thus the reactions of others to you. Negative thoughts will attempt to creep in and you must expend energy to deflect them and replace them as they attempt to interrupt your positive cycle. Pay attention to the positives and ignore, forget or replace the negatives and your internal energy will begin to cycle in a positive direction and negative cycles will be reversed. You will begin to emanate positive rather than negative energy. Focus your Chi on each moment of each day, of each person, of each situation. Pay attention and change each thought and action in a conscious way. In Zen, it is eating when you eat and sleeping when you sleep.

Be where you are. Organize your attention on the situation at hand. This organization is positive, the disorganization of not paying attention and not focusing yourself on the situation is negative energy and yields negative results. Stress, negativity and discord begin to replace positive Chi when you interrupt your focus.

Many of us feel stress because our body is in one place while our mind and focus is elsewhere. This phenomenon separates mind from body. It interrupts your spirit and disrupts any positive Chi you might have been experiencing. The whole notion of multi-tasking in today's modern age is an interruption of focus and a separation of mind and body from the same task. The result is that you perform no task well. The human can only perform one physical task at a time and that task requires mental oversight. If the mind is elsewhere while the body is attempting to perform a task then the task will not be effective or successful. When the mind attempts to perform two or more tasks, it cannot perform them in parallel.

Consciously we can only manage one task in one instant. We delude ourselves into thinking that we can multi-task, when all we are doing is one task at a time. We are lining tasks up one after the other, or worse, we attempt a portion of one for an instant, then a portion of another, for another instant or two, then back to the first, then the second, then possibly adding on a third. If any one of these tasks requires some degree of extended concentration beyond a stolen instant or two that task is in danger of failing and generally will. Likewise, the body begins to fatigue and become stressed due to the separation from mind in these ill-fated attempts to multi-task. As the monks instruct, eat when you eat, walk when you walk.

The spirit is most at peace when the mind and body are connected working in harmony and in the same place at the same time. Try this and you will see that the positive energy expended to maintain focus yields positive energy. The negative energy generated as you allow your focus to shift elsewhere yields negative energy around you.

Your meditation should focus on conscious identification of what positive and negative roles you play in the lives of those around you. Replace the negative ones, visualize the positive roles that you do or will play. Meditate to visualize the martial skills that you seek. Visualize, in your mind's eye, yourself performing techniques the way you wish to perform them.

Meditation position

Meditation begins with breathing and relaxing. Deep, clean, full breathing provides the positive energy from oxygen coming in and removing the negative energy of breathing's byproduct of carbon dioxide. As you begin your meditation, you focus on purging your body of the waste products when you exhale and move toward purging your mind of negativity. As you purge your mind, you purge your entire being of negativity and you begin to ground yourself and connect mind and body to affect your spirit and to generate positive Chi while you meditate. Release the ego and desire and the want of being able to perform and simply focus on seeing yourself absorbing new knowledge and new understanding of what you seek.

Awareness

Awareness of what your opponent is doing means that you have not quite advanced to the level of actually understanding what he is doing. As you improve your focus and ability to relax more even in combat, your awareness will improve which will lead to better understanding and perception of your opponent and his intentions.

see --->aware---->understand---->perceive opponent's intention = determine your intention

- Seeing leads to awareness.
- Awareness leads to understating.
- Understanding leads to perception of your opponent's intentions.
- Perception of your opponent's intentions leads to determining your intentions.

Awareness comes from being relaxed and removing tension. When you are relaxed, your mind is able to be more aware. This makes focus possible. You must understand and practice these things. As you are better able to perceive your opponent and determine his intentions, you will be able to better formulate your intentions and respond accordingly.

Energy

Train so that you are always ready. Eat well so that you will be generally healthy, but be able and ready to fight without having eaten or prepared. That is the nature of truly being ready for self-defense or any type of combat.

- - - - - - - - -

Food and vitamins are essential to proper functioning of the body, but be able to function well at all times and do not focus on hunger, pain, discomforts of climate, other distractions or fatigue. You must be able to go on even with these annoyances and distractions. Your survival may depend upon it.

Energy is a precious resource of the body. You must be conservative with it. In a prolonged encounter, you will need all you can muster. A novice or intermediate student will be brimming with energy and adrenalin. They are excited or apprehensive about sparring or having an encounter. We all are. The difference is that the more advanced student must learn control. Discipline yourself to relax so that you will not burn vital energy and tire quickly. Then the energy will be available when you need a quick burst in a dramatic moment. When you are relaxed, you will burn less energy and be able to focus more effectively.

Mushin: Not-Thinking

The Japanese call this "Mushin" which loosely translates as "No mind." The idea behind Mushin is to work to be in a state of not thinking, but of sensing and reacting. It has been said that the ability to think is a great gift. However, consider that the ability not to think is at least an equally valuable thing.

Do not always think. Just simply experience and take in things. Let the mind rest. As I have said, when you are trying too hard or thinking too much, it will not come to you, whatever you are attempting. Learn to let go and stop seeking it. Then it will be there.

Try taking a walk by a lake or in the woods or any place that might be peaceful or scenic. Take notice of everything, but do not think about the things that you notice. Conclude nothing, merely observe and attach no meaning or significance to anything, simply be aware of its existence and try control your mind so that you generate no thoughts. The mind naturally wants to stimulate itself to the next level of thinking about what it has observed. Do not allow this to happen because these thoughts are distracting you from being able to simply observe and be completely aware of your environment. If you are distracted by your own thoughts such as how beautiful a flower may be, you will miss many things in your surroundings because you just became distracted by your thoughts. This awareness is essential for survival. Unnecessary thoughts can degrade your ability to perceive your opponent or the dangers of a situation.

Practice not thinking ... this is simply being. It is harder than it seems. Not thinking is being thoughtful of things without thinking.

It is awareness without analysis. It is simply taking in without concluding anything.

Visual Skill: Vision and Seeing

Anyone who has eyes that function can see. Seeing and vision are simple mechanical functions of the body. Vision serves a greater purpose however, to the fighter. Properly trained and focused, vision relays the message of the opponent's intentions and that can mean life or death.

The beginner uses vision to see his opponent. The experienced martial artist uses vision to perceive his opponent and his intentions.

Field of View

Know your field of view. Be aware of everything in it. Do not react to everything or you will often be misdirected and your intentions will be incoherent to you because you do not properly perceive what is in your field of view.

When you perceive what is in your field of view, you will know what to do. When something is in your field of view, you do not have to look directly at it to realize that it might be a threat. Looking at something takes time and it may not have been worth looking at.

Keep your attention focused on what is most important. By being aware within your field of view, you can see things without looking. By doing this you can prioritize what is most important without looking at everything. Learn to see without looking, this saves time.

Practice staring at a fixed point; without altering your point of focus then try to notice how much is visible in your periphery. What can you actually see without looking directly at it? Become more conscious of what is in your peripheral vision and be able to see consciously these things without turning your head or eyes in their direction. Then when you spar, you can focus on the center of your opponent's body, which will make it possible to see both his or her hands and their feet in your peripheral vision. If you watch their feet and anticipate a kick, you will not necessarily see a hand strike that is coming from the upper regions because it is outside of your field of view. Your peripheral vision is actually more sensitive to movement which gives you a built in survival skill, use it.

Understanding

Understanding what your opponent is doing begins with seeing them do it. When you see them do something and you recognize what that movement is and what it means to you then you understand your opponent. If you understand what they are doing without having yet acquired enough experience to know what you must do in response, then you do not yet truly perceive them.

Remember if you perceive your opponent accurately, then your intentions and movements will be one, driven by that perception. If you have only reached the level of understanding without yet being able to perceive what you must do, your intentions will be void because without perception, you will not really know what to do and your response, if any, will be misguided and ineffective.

Movement without perception does not have intention. Therefore, it is wasted. You must perceive what you must do to be effective against an opponent.

Perception

Perception is seeing the same thing that a beginner sees, but understanding what you are seeing and knowing what must happen next. Perception requires vision, knowledge, experience and understanding. Simple vision does not. Perception is a cognitive act rather than sensory.

The beginner may see the opponent but does not fully understand what he must to do respond effectively to a kick, and does not formulate a plan or employ any tactics to counter or avoid the attack.

To summarize:

- The beginner sees his opponent.
- The intermediate student sees, but adds understanding of what his opponent is doing.
- The experienced martial artist perceives his opponent; knowing what he must do in response. This response is your intention driven by your perception. This perception allows your intentions to be the same as your movements; they are one in the same.

The beginner is not yet able to make the connection where intentions and movement are the same because he does not yet have the middle component of understanding what his opponent is doing. The beginner is unable to perceive what he must do.

The beginner is only able to see his opponent. The rest will happen over time. Until he matures, a beginner will simply know that he must do something, but will not know what and he will not understand what his opponent is doing.

None of this, however, is strategy. Perception and intention lead to choice of specific techniques, movements, actions and responses, which are merely tactical adjustments. Strategy, as you will see later is a larger concept involving the combination of many tactics to achieve larger aims than simply knowing how to react to simple movements.

The intermediate student recognizes that the opponent is preparing for an attack (kick) before it happens or just as it starts; the advanced student recognizes the attack and already has several responses formulated and waiting.

Purpose of Technique

Know the purpose of a strike and the appropriate targets for the strike. This should be obvious, but to the beginner and even the advanced student it is not always so. You may know how and when to throw a technique, but you must understand the purpose of the technique. Imitating kicks and punches in a kata does not teach you their true purpose.

It is unpleasant to think about, but all martial arts techniques (except those, which control, avoid or re-direct without causing permanent damage) are designed so that you may do some harm to your opponent.

Your job as a martial artist is to understand what damage you are trying to inflict with each technique and how this damage occurs. If you do not understand the kind of damage possible with a given technique, then you are a danger to your training partners and yet you may not be enough of a danger to a real enemy. Therefore, the purpose of a technique is a double-edged sword. Understand it well.

Learning and Knowing

To learn a technique or a strategy is not the same thing as knowing it. When you know something, you can apply it and put it to good use in the way in which you need. If you have learned something new, you must still practice it until it becomes natural and subconscious, then you know it.

- - - - - - - - - -

There are many ways to learn something. Learn by listening to your instructor. Learn by watching your instructor demonstrate. Learn by trying and doing something yourself.

Learn by failing. Failure at something is one of the greatest teachers. You are not actually failing, however, until you quit. If you keep trying and go on to master your challenge, and then you have succeeded and truly learned something.

We often learn best from our failures or mistakes because we carry the memory of their pain. Pain is more easily remembered as a reminder of how NOT to do something than someone's explanation of how TO do something.

Openings and Opportunities

A beginning student is full of open, vulnerable places if you know how to recognize them. An opening is only an opening if you recognize it as such.

With an expert there can be many openings also, if you know how to find them. If your opponent is skilled, he covers his openings, making them hard to reach. The openings are still there if you know how to get to them.

When an opening does not appear to exist, then you must create it. Again, you must simply know what to look for or what target you wish to strike, and then develop a strategy to expose that target to your weapon of choice. Pull down their guard; make them react to create an opening. You will see that it was there all the time. Now strike before he closes what you opened.

The attacker, in black, is pulling down her opponent's guard to create an opening to the face so that she can execute a punch.

The front foot of the opponent is vulnerable to a sweep and takedown and the front knee is vulnerable to a kick.

The better the fighter, the less obvious the openings and the more difficult it is to draw their guard away. The key to victory is in finding or making these openings. If you wait for one to appear, it may never come.

When you execute deception through fakes and distraction, you aim to expose an enemy's openings or weaknesses. We will discuss this more later.

Rhythm

Develop your own rhythm as you fight, but do not allow your opponent to interrupt your rhythm. Even if he does, take it in stride. Strive to interrupt and ruin his rhythm.

When he is busy pursuing you with a single-minded intent to defeat you, then you must jump in the middle of his rhythm, vary your timing and distance to confuse him and ruin his plans. Make him respond to you rather than you responding to him.

Your own rhythm could be that you vary your pace, or you maintain a constant pace. Either way, fit your opponent's advances into your rhythm while you upset his. As you learn to read your opponent's movement and intentions better, you will be able to preempt and intercept his techniques and strategies.

Grappling and Chokes

Some styles of martial arts include grappling techniques others exclude grappling. If you are in tight quarters and are unable to execute a kick or a strong punch, you may have to use grappling techniques.

Grappling, with its holds, arm-bars, joint manipulation and joint locks should be part of your martial arts training. It makes you a more robust opponent and understanding grappling will help you defend against it as well.

Most fights begin as shoving matches or as grappling or wrestling situations and yet many traditional styles ignore this, why? Grappling can be a little more involved than basic kicking and punching. Some styles argue that as long as you can keep your opponent at a distance you can kick or punch, but what if you are caught by surprise with a grab from behind. This is a grappling situation. Without knowledge of grappling, you are at a loss and may panic when your training fails you.

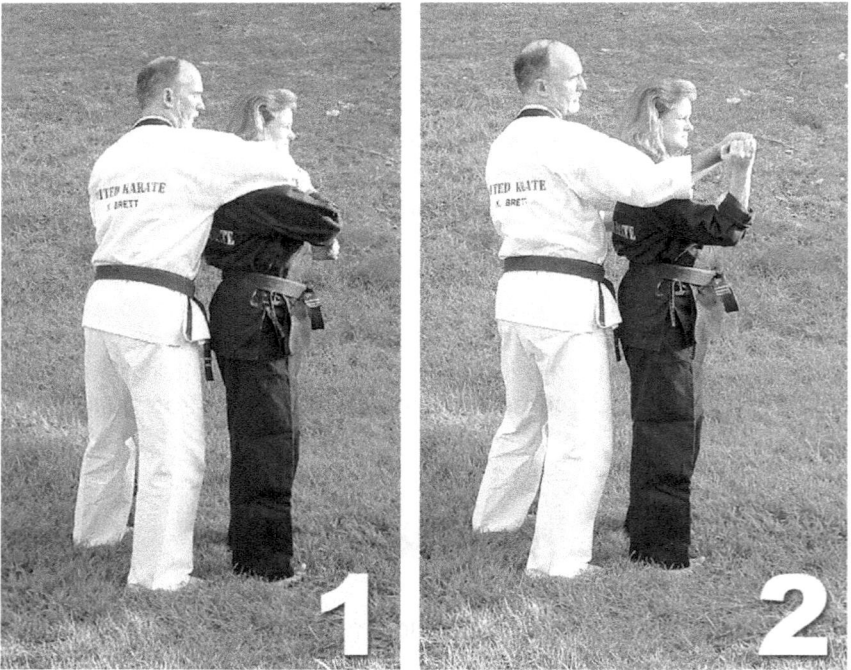

The defender in black uses a wrist manipulation technique to unwrap the opponent's stronger grip.

Next, she converts her handgrip to a controlling arm-bar for pain compliance. If necessary, she could break her opponent's elbow or wrist.

Learn grappling, it is essential for close range fighting. Grappling has legal advantages. If you can subdue an opponent without causing damage, you may not be liable for injuries that you might cause by other, more destructive techniques such as kicks.

Kicking

There are many beautiful and deadly kicks in different styles of martial arts. Like grappling, punching and joint manipulation, kicking has its place and it should have a place in your library of techniques.

Kicks need not be head-level to be effective. The most effective kicks are those, which you can deliver without putting your balance or footing at risk. The more unstable the surface, on which you are standing, such as ice, snow, gravel, the lower the kicks should be. Aim for vital targets, groin, side of the knee, thighs, ankles, bridge of the foot.

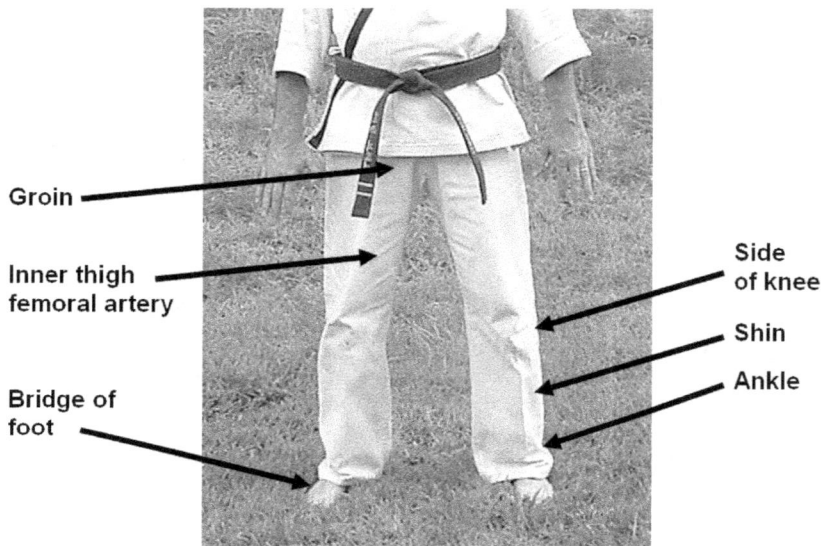

Common targets below the belt

You can cause much damage with kicks below the belt. You need not risk falling or being pushed off balance by trying to kick someone in the head. Conversely, with enough experience and expertise, you can deliver high kicks to the head or upper body with devastating power. Timing, distance, power, speed, experience and environment are all key factors, not to mention the nature of your opponent.

As with all other techniques, learn a wide variety of kicks, preferably the more practical ones. Learn which targets are most appropriate for which kicks and what situations are most appropriate. Practice kicking drills for timing, speed, flexibility, power and distance. Keep these skills sharp, as with all other techniques, they are part of your total arsenal. Have them ready and waiting. You will know the right time to use them.

Low kicks are the most effective. Kicks that are waist-level or below are safer for the person executing the kick. A higher kicking target will result in the kicker being unable to generate as much force as with a lower kick due to the effects of gravity. The kicker will also have less balance. Therefore the most powerful and stable kicks are those that aim for waist level and below.

Punching

You should study punches or punching types of techniques in depth to become a well-rounded martial artist. Basic boxing is more primitive and limited than most martial systems, but there is value still. An effective lead punch, uppercut or jab can add significant depth to your arsenal of techniques and you can combine them with various kicks or other more traditional martial arts techniques.

Learn how to use hand combinations. Learn the targets for which a boxer aims. Even if you are not a fan of boxing techniques, you will at least know what to expect from an opponent who is. Boxing ability adds to you total skill set. You can use it effectively against marital artists who are not good at close range fighting and tend to rely on distance techniques such as kicks. Add boxing skills and knowledge to your studies. This will add a new dimension of versatility to your abilities.

Temple

Jaw

Kidneys

Chin "button"

Solar plexus

Typical boxing targets on the body. Note that boxers do not strike below the belt

Hand Techniques

There is a wide variety of hand techniques available to the martial artist. You are not limited to simply using the fist to punch. You can use hand techniques for effective strikes to the eyes, throat, nose, groin and other vital points. Every martial arts style has its favored set of techniques. Learning a good variety of them will improve your overall arsenal and give you additional options in

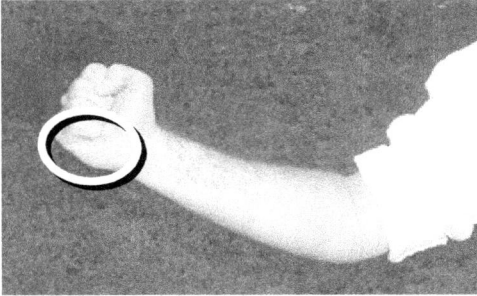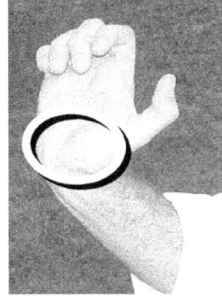

Hammer fist   Palm heel

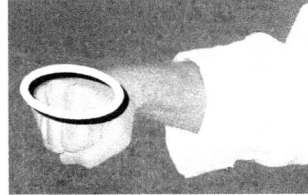

Ridge hand   Punch

*Various weapons of the hand. Circles indicate the
strike point of the weapon.*

There are also many uses for the elbow. Elbow strikes can be
used to strike the stomach, the face, jaw and the spine and other
targets.

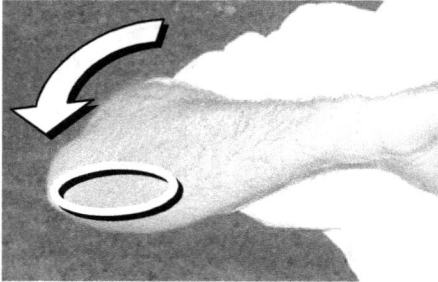

Sideways elbow strike   Upward elbow strike

Elbow strikes: Strike points are circled. Arrows indicate the
path of movement of the arm.

Blocking and Deflection

Not everything is worth blocking. Blocking usually takes more time
and energy than simply avoiding a strike so that a block is not
even necessary. Blocking or deflecting one technique can also
leave you exposed for a rapid follow-up technique from your
opponent. So be judicious in what you choose to block.

You can study many types of blocks, parries and interceptions.
There are two types of blocks: the hard block and the soft block.
With the hard block, you strike the opponent's weapon. This may
be his leg that is attempting to kick or his arm that is attempting to
punch. A hard block will usually strike perpendicular to the path of
the weapon, slicing in a head-on manner. This type of block may
damage your opponent's weapon and possibly your own. The
hard block is the most natural and usually covers a shorter
distance than the soft block. With a hard block, you exert more
energy than a soft block and generally require more strength.
There is also a greater chance of injury with a hard block.

A soft block is the way of intercepting the opponent from a diagonal or circular motion. The advantage here is that you do not strike nearly as hard. You simply deflect the weapon from an angle or use a circular motion. Since you are already cutting off their advancing weapon, you can turn your diagonal block into an immediate strike once you have intercepted their offensive move.

There are many other soft blocks from the softer styles. These include the scooping blocks that are usually circular. They intercept at a diagonal or sometimes perpendicular to the path of the strike as do the hard blocks, but instead of stopping the weapon as a hard block does, they carry the weapon away in a scooping or sweeping motion.

The defender, in white, is using a hard perpendicular block to strike the punching arm of the attacker.

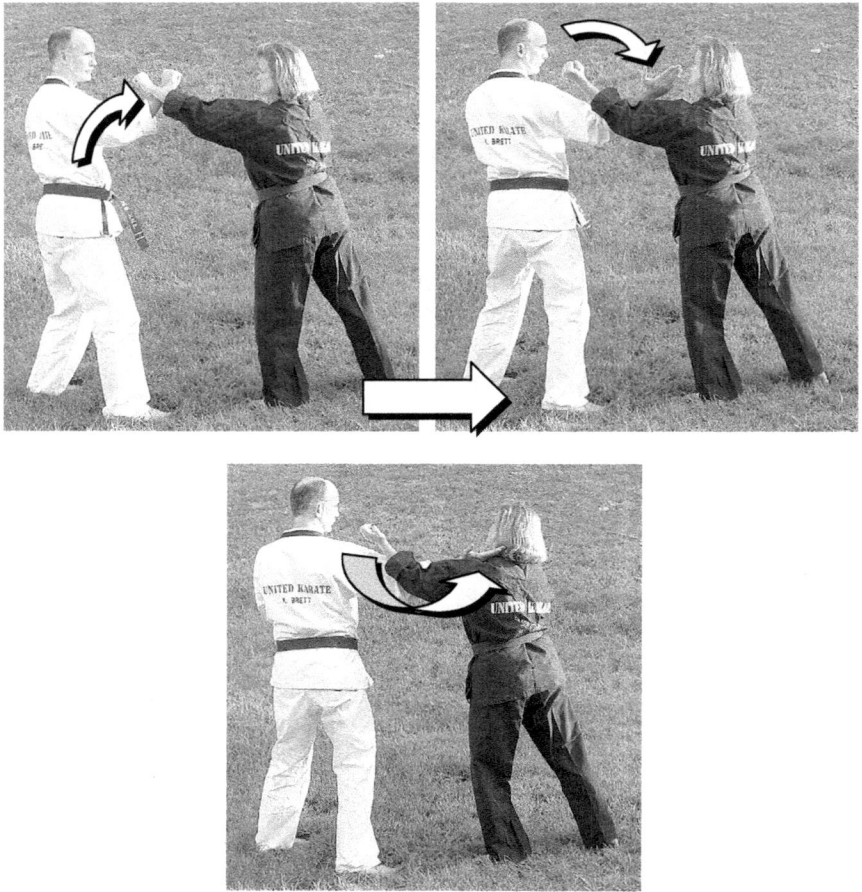

A diagonal deflection block with a follow up chop to the neck.

The defender, in white, is stepping off the line of attack and blocking the punch with a soft scooping arm block to carry away a punch.

With your blocks and parries, do not simply study style. Every style of martial art has its blocks, counters, parries and strikes. The specific type or style of block does not matter. Different styles of martial arts tend to adopt different mechanics of motion based on their creator's preferences and philosophy of combat. What is important is whether it works. To make it work reliably, you must understand the motion of your opponent's strike and your own

---

mechanics of motion. Then the block, the strike and the style of martial arts will be irrelevant. You will simply be applying the general mechanics of motion as you choose.

Study and understand the motion and mechanics of how your body moves. Different styles simply put motion to use in a variety of ways to affect a block or strike. As you begin to understand motion, body mechanics and anatomy, you will better understand how to make blocks really work no matter what the style. You will simply be learning how the body is able to move rather than memorizing specific movements.

Learning only the style without understanding mechanics of motion or the mechanics of the body is simply imitation. There is no real knowledge in imitation. It is only a matter of appearances. An advanced student can recognize imitation or a lack of real understanding in the technique of a less skilled martial artist.

Angles

A straight line is direct, but it is also obvious. Every beginner goes straight for the target like a bull charging a matador. The experienced fighter attacks indirectly from angles or in circular patterns which are expected from an experienced fighter, but then switches to straight lines occasionally for surprise.

An attack from an angle can allow you to move out of the direct path of your opponent's weapons or line of attack, while actually moving your weapon closer to them at the same time. While they are still facing forward, where you used to be, you are now beside or behind them and it is too late for them.

Angles such as a diagonal or some other oblique angle are useful for blocks and deflection as mentioned earlier.

"In the beginner's mind, there are many possibilities. In the mind of the expert there are few."

- Japanese Emperor Mazda

Ground Fighting

Most fights end up on the ground. When they do, what happens next depends upon who is the better ground fighter. If you have no training in ground fighting and your opponent has even one single effective technique in his arsenal that he is able to execute against you, you are at a serious disadvantage.

As I mentioned with grappling, you must learn these things. Ground fighting is a part of grappling. Grappling can take place either standing or it can take place on the ground. Many of the same grappling techniques that work in an upright manner will also work on the ground. This is your starting point. You will also notice that you can apply many of the grappling techniques from the kata while you are pinned on the ground. You are simply in a different position and the techniques might require some slight modification, but this gives you a good starting point.

The defender, in black, is pinned down, but uses a dissolve to the bone, followed by a chop to the elbow with a hand wedge to stress the elbow joint providing leverage to roll her opponent over while maintaining a folded arm bar for control.

Your goal in all training is to reduce or eliminate disadvantages. Give yourself advantages by making your training as comprehensive as possible. Study fighting techniques and methods for all types of opponents and situations. Even if you have not studied a particular type of opponent or situation in detail, the mere fact that you have diverse training experience will likely help you adapt to a new situation more rapidly than someone who is strictly traditional and staid in his or her training and thinking.

U.S. Marines practice ground fighting in the sand as part of the Marine Corps Martial Arts Program.

Takedowns and Sweeps

Takedowns and sweeps are often included in grappling studies. You can accomplish them from grappling maneuvers. They are useful because they can put your opponent down and reduce the potential threat.

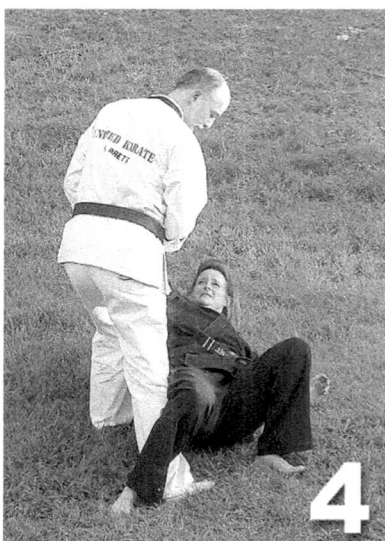

The defender, in white, uses a wrist manipulation to twist the opponent over and down to the ground.

If your opponent is not skilled in ground fighting and your sweep or takedown brings both of you down in a flurry of grabs, you will still have the advantage, because by bringing them down to the ground where you are experienced, you have just brought them down into your territory. This gives you the advantage, but only if you are properly trained.

Pressure Points and Dim Mak

Like grappling, the study of pressure points and vital points can provide an additional advantage. This area is often ignored, but can have great value. Study the effective use of pressure points. They are another way of subduing your opponent without necessarily causing permanent damage.

There may be just that one situation or position in which a pressure point technique might be appropriate or more effective or desirable than a punch or kick or other technique. Having options gives you the advantage. The less damage caused the better unless you are truly fighting for your life. You must decide where you are on the force continuum and whether lethal force is appropriate.

The Chinese have discovered that there are dozens of pressure points all over the body. We commonly know these as acupuncture points. The Chinese discovered that pressure applied to these pressure points in just the right manner caused different effects on various functions of the body. Some effects include muscle weakness, dizziness, loss of consciousness and even death.

These pressure points were studied and combined with techniques that evolved into methods for achieving tactical advantages of opponents. The art of Dim Mak, meaning Death Touch, was developed in China. This art consists of various touches and strikes that can either cause instant death or delayed death. The Chinese believed that the body contains a series of lines or meridians with various points along these meridians that are known as pressure points. Where multiple meridians intersect or overlap the pressure points are more significant and generally make better targets for different types of attacks. Some of these meridians correspond to nerves, some to various arteries and some to internal organs. When affected in the right way, changes to the autonomic nervous system, circulatory system or the proper function of internal organs can be affected resulting in extreme pain, serious injury or death.

You need not understand all of these pressure points, which can take a lifetime to study, but knowledge of a few of them and how to target them is studied by many martial artists to provide a few worthwhile targets and options in their arsenals.

Weapons

Many schools and instructors have no experience with or knowledge of weapons. They assume that all martial arts involve hand-to-hand combat. This could not be further from the truth. Weapons techniques represent at least half of martial arts.

There are dozens of primary martial arts weapons and hundreds of less common, but nonetheless useful and effective weapons. Weapons and their techniques have evolved over the centuries side by side with unarmed techniques.

If for no other reason than to preserve their heritage, you should study weapons. However, there are many other reasons for the study of classical weapons. All well designed martial arts weapons are an extension of the users hand or arm. They are designed or used in such a manner as to become a part of the person carrying them.

Defending against a strike from a bo-staff.

The very soul of the Japanese Samurai, for example, is the Katana - the long sword. The Samurai went nowhere without this blade. The Japanese Ninja, on the other hand, were well versed in a wide array of weapons and means of waging warfare with them; everything from hand-made explosives to grappling hooks to short, straight versions of the Samurai Katana.

The study of weapons can begin with intermediate students. At the intermediate level, students have begun to develop the rudiments of knowledge about movement, open hand technique and physical conditioning. At this point, it is possible to begin their

---

study of weapons so that they may begin to see how to integrate a weapon into their arsenal of techniques and how the weapon becomes a natural extension of them. It will also be important to an intermediate student to begin to understand how to block and deflect various types of strikes or blows with primitive weapons such as a club or even a pool queue.

A student can begin to see how to move with and without a weapon. They can begin to understand movement and body mechanics better through the study of the motion of a weapon. They also begin to understand how to use the striking or blocking power of the weapon to cause damage in the same way that they begin to learn how to use the striking or blocking ability of their arms or legs.

Many common martial arts weapons were derived from everyday objects in the countries and times in which they evolved. Farmers used nunchakus to beat stalks of rice. Rice farmers used kamas to cut rice. Farmers often used Sais as pins for ox carts. The bo-staff had many everyday uses such as carrying pails of water or dirt.

Typical martial arts weapons may not be legal to carry today as they were in previous centuries, but through their study, the martial artist can learn to adapt and utilize everyday objects of this century for the same purposes – self-defense. This is where it is important to study weapons of opportunity.

Effective Techniques

Martial arts systems are built upon many techniques for protecting against and causing temporary or permanent pain, damage or injury to an aggressor. For these techniques to be effective in self-defense situation, the martial artist must know what damage a technique can inflict on an opponent. Most martial arts schools do not teach this because their instructors do not know it themselves.

Knowledge of the medical implications of various martial arts techniques is crucial for effective self-defense.

Knowledge of basic anatomy and the physiology of movement is important in helping the martial artist learn how to execute the technique so that it will have the desired medical consequence. This is not a pleasant subject, but neither is assault, murder or rape, which of course is what a martial artist hopes to prevent or avoid.

Overextension or Hyperextension and Hyper flexion

When I first learned to throw kicks and punches, our instructors taught us to extend fully our arms or legs and "lock" the joint out. This has the effect of overextending the tendons and ligaments in the joint and leads to strains, sprains and painful joints. In fact, full extension of the leg or arm in a kick or punch is completely unrealistic because at the point of full extension all power in the technique has been dissipated.

The further out the kick of punch travels from the point of origin, the less power it has behind it. Hyperextension is the point at which the tendons and joint ligaments are extended beyond their normal extension and serious damage to this soft tissue occurs. This type of damage is typical in ankle and knee sprains and whiplash injuries.

Strength Apex

The strength apex is the point in a punch or kick where the technique is capable of generating the maximum amount of force. Simple geometry governs this fact. One hundred and twenty

---

degrees is the strength apex for a kick or punch or essentially any arm or leg technique. When the elbow or knee is at an angle of 120 degrees the muscles of the upper and lower leg or the upper and lower arm are at a point of balance in flexion and extension where they have equal power and both sets of muscles can be applied toward the technique equally to generate more power.

The key to making the 120-degree strength apex work in your favor is that the technique will have its maximum effectiveness in terms of the power generated when the target is struck at the point that the arm or leg reaches is strength apex. Any point of impact before or after the magic number of 120 degrees will have a diminished level of power.

Strength apex for front-kick

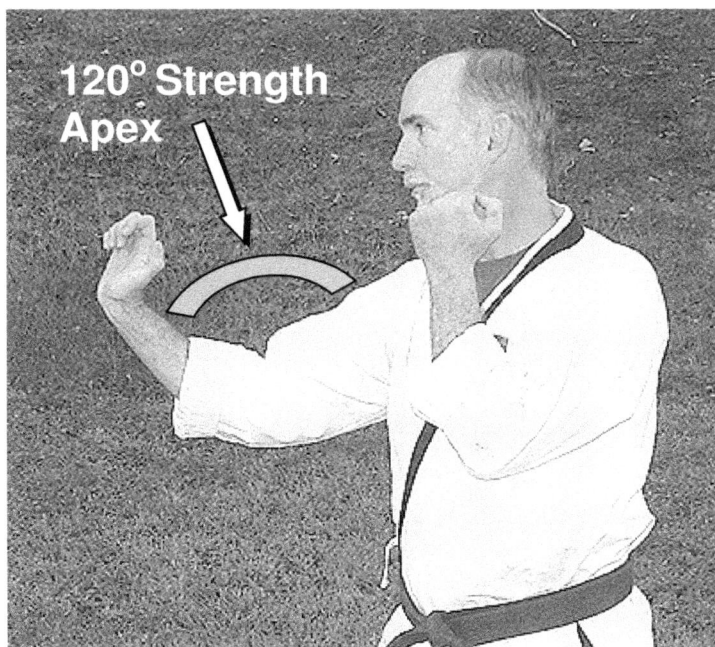

Strength apex for palm heel

If you notice martial artists who break bricks and cinderblocks, they wind up their punches and kicks and walk through the technique much the same was a golfer lines up at the tee and gets himself properly aligned and throws a practice swing. They are both checking the alignment and angle of their technique.

When a hand technique or kick is executed so that the point of impact occurs at the strength apex, the technique will be capable of generating maximum power while still having adequate force after reaching the strength apex to penetrate through or into the target.

Strength apex for sidekick

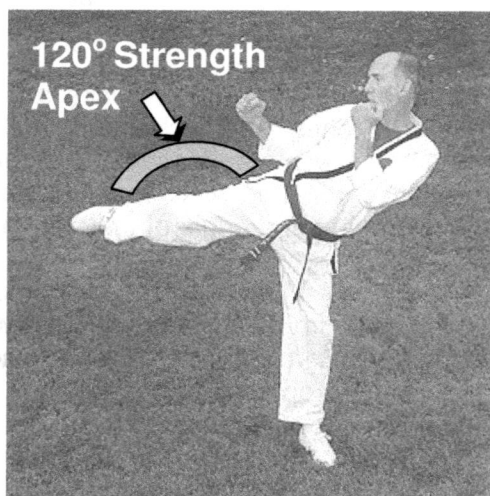

Strength apex for roundkick

For example, it requires significant force to break a stack of boards, but in order to break the last board, the martial artist must still have some remaining power in the technique and room for full extension into and past the last board. The key to successful breaking is not to hit the boards, but to penetrate beyond them. That is why when practicing punches and kicks in a kata or in the air without having an opponent or target bag it is bad technique to extend fully the punch or kick. The hand or foot technique should be pulled just short of full extension so that the elbow or knee remains slightly bent. This will prevent all of the power of the technique and shock from being transferred to the joint. In a real combat situation and effective strike would not transfer its impact to the joint, but rather to the point of impact on the opponent's body.

Effective Stances

Now that we understand the benefits of the strength apex, we can see that it is easier to maintain balance in a stance or move rapidly from a stance such as a traditional front-stance or back-stance to some other position by taking advantage of the strength apex.

Front and back stances are two of the most common and natural stances in many styles of martial arts. Yet the true effectiveness of the stance eludes many students and instructors. Very low, deep stances look dramatic and impressive. They make us think of a serious Samurai warrior deeply set in his defensive or offensive posture close to the earth, solid in his positioning and seemingly immovable.

Unfortunately, the lower and wider the stance, the less balance the person actually has. Position a student into a front stance, one in a very deep stance, well beyond the 120-degree strength apex of the front knee and with his or her feet approximately twice shoulder width apart. Then stand perpendicular to the student and gently push them on the shoulder perpendicular to the direction they are facing, they will fall over. Their stance is built on faulty geometry.

Now position the student so that the front knee is at the strength apex of 120 degrees and the feet are only slightly wider than shoulder width. Push the student with the same force as before and you will see that they go nowhere and it takes much more effort to push the student from their stance. The same concept applies to the back-stance.

Point of Origin

Motion from the point of origin is a martial arts concept that refers to the idea that techniques in some instances must be executed so rapidly or with so little telegraphing of intent, that there is not time to wind-up and fully rotate the hips or fully contract the arm or leg to execute the technique. To illustrate, you can execute a hand technique such as a ridge-had to the groin effectively by simply leaving out the wind-up of the arm. Add hip rotation without winding up the hip. For example if you are executing a right-hand ridge hand, then rotate the hips and torso to the left rapidly in a sudden twisting motion and whip the ridge hand forward as the hip rotation reaches its maximum speed.

The hip rotation adds rotational force (torque) to the hand technique augmenting the strength of the technique beyond simply using the arm muscles by themselves. The technique travels a shorter distance than if there was a pre-rotation wind-up of the hips and torso, yet you can generate significant power to make the technique more effective.

The defender, in black, strikes from the point of origin. Her right hand does not wind up or pull back and her hips do not wind back. She twists her hip forward to the right, her knew and shoulder for extra torque and power and executes a right ridge hand strike to the groin while simultaneously dropping her weight into a stance to add the force of gravity to her strike. For added protection, she also raises her left hand to protect her face from any strike.

Gravitational Force

To make techniques like the groin strike or a forearm down-block more effective, add gravitational force to the linear and rotational forces described above. Imagine stepping onto a scale to weigh yourself. Suppose the scale reads 180 pounds. Now step off the scale and jump onto it. You will likely see the needle or the digital readout on the scale jump to something like 300 pounds. You have just added the effects of gravity to your weight reading on the scale.

Now imagine executing a board break or a downward ax kick or even a punch with the added force of gravity. As you throw a punch, you use the linear force of your arm muscles, the rotational strength of your hips and torso and the gravitational force of dropping your body position from a relatively upright position to a stance-like position where your knees are close to the strength apex as the technique is completed. In other words, rise up slightly prior to executing the technique, rotate to wind-up for the rotational force, drop down, and twist simultaneously as you release the technique.

These forces combined can significantly increase the power of anyone's technique. This will all take time to practice, refine and internalize. Do it often, isolate the individual forces, and practice just those elements of a technique until they come naturally and feel natural.

This front punch in a front stance begins in a very moderate front stance that is not too low. Notice in the second frame where the shoulder and hip rotate backward to wind up and the puncher rises up slightly. The depth of the stance also lessens some during the windup.

In frame three the hip, right knee and shoulder all rotate back to unwind toward the target. The stance re-forms and in frame four the puncher drops down suddenly in a lower stance than in frame one with hips, right knee and shoulder pivoted forward to penetrate through the target. This punch combines the torque power from the windup followed with the explosive rotation of the body in frame three and four with dropping the weight into the stance in frame four. All these factors combine provide a significant power boost at the point of impact of the punch.

Telegraphing: Japanese vs. Okinawan

The Japanese conquered the Okinawan Islands in 1600. The Japanese did not allow the Okinawans to practice martial arts unless they were teaching them to Japanese Samurai. The Japanese confiscated all weapons in Okinawa. The Okinawans responded by adapting farm implements as weapons. Tonfa, which we know today as police night sticks were originally used for grinding rice. Nunchakus were used for beating stalks of rice. Sais were used as pins for ox carts and Kammas were used to slash and harvest rice. All of these tools were turned into highly effective weapons and practiced in secret.

Legend has it that when Okinawans did practice karate, they taught the Samurai that their stances should be low and wide. Of course, this made it difficult for the Samurai to move and actually decreased their balance and left them exposed and vulnerable. Later forms of Japanese Karate still incorporate these low stances as they were learned and passed on by the ruling Samurai.

Low front stance. This stance is so low that It is very difficult to move from this position to another. It is also very unstable and makes it difficult to maintain balance.

A very low horse-riding stance. This stance is also too low to make movement to another stance or position easy to do without tipping off your opponent.

A very low back stance. This stance is very unstable and is very difficult to transition out of. Despite the low, wide base, your balance in this stance is also very poor.

Types of Impact

There are three types of force or impact when executing any type of strike:

Penetration or displacing strikes: These strikes aim to go deep into the target with the objective of causing deep damage and disruption.

Penetration or displacement strike to the solar plexus to move the opponent back ward.

Shock-impact strikes: These strikes penetrate only slightly and should be pulled back instantly which results in a shock wave of force traveling into the target.

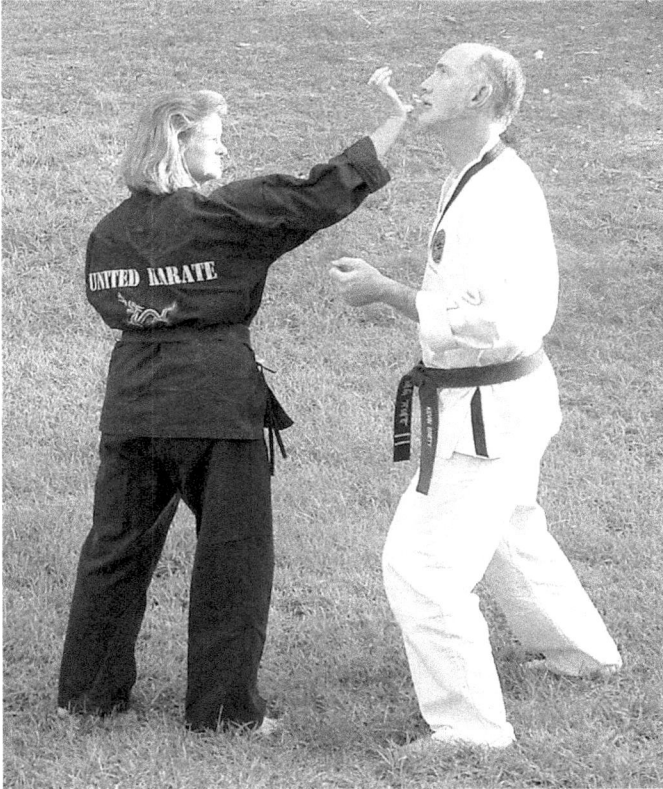

Shock-impact strike to the face.

Whipping strikes: These types of strikes are purely a surface strike. Examples of these would be a whip to the eyes with the backside of one's fingers, or a quick whip or wrist flick of the fingers toward the groin.

Whipping strike to the face and eyes.

Softening and Finishing Techniques

Many people are familiar with volleyball where a common strategy is to "set up" the other side for a spike of the ball. Three taps of the ball are allowed to get it to the other side. The final tap is the spike, which is intended to be a dunk on the other side of the net that is ideally irretrievable by the other side. This strike is the final blow to score a point.

Self-defense situations work in much the same way. You may not subdue an assailant or defeat them with a single well-placed blow. Generally, it is a safe bet that you will need several preparatory moves or strikes to distract, disorient and soften up the opponent. Once you have executed several techniques in rapid succession, you can issue a final finishing blow.

One example of this strategy would be if an assailant grabbed you by the throat from behind. He has you in a tight grip and you are unable to muscle your way free. The ultimate objective is to free yourself from the grip. To accomplish this, you might strike down to the groin with a vertical chop, and then stomp down on the bridge of one of your opponent's feet. Then maybe you can repeat the strike to the groin with a backward scoop kick to the groin, then possibly a foot strike to the top of the knee with a scraping downward motion along the shinbone.

Finally, at this point it should be possible that with the pain inflicted on your opponent, you would be able to reach up with one hand and unpeel the grip of the opponent's outermost hand by turning it outward against the direction that the wrist turns. Maintaining the grip as you peel the wrist away begins to break the grip and continuing the outward turn of the opponent's wrist begins to bring him to his knees. This technique works because all of the initial preparation movement causes the opponent to loose grip, focus and strength due to the pain inflicted. Now a weaker defender can use leverage to overcome a stronger opponent.

Martial Exercises vs. Traditional Calisthenics

Most martial arts schools begin their training classes with a warm up period containing traditional calisthenics; jumping jacks, push ups, jogging in place and the like. My approach to warming up a class is that everything you do should have some martial application. You are studying martial arts and the goal of improving your skill is to increase your odds of survival on the street or wherever you happen to be. When I have a group conduct warm-ups, they are practicing for survival, even in a fun way. Here are a few examples of how cardio vascular, strengthening and conditioning exercises can be accomplished in a more combat-realistic setting:

Rather than do push-ups, I have students to punch push-ups. Each time the student comes up in the push-up, they throw a punch forward toward and opponent who may be on the ground with them.

Rather than do jumping jacks, I have students to punching jacks where they throw a punch on each landing while holding their hands in a boxing position ready to defend themselves.

Punching jacks

I have students simply crawl on their belly from one end of the dojo to the other and back. Sometimes we string lines of rope the length of the dojo and tell them that their head must stay low so that it does not touch the rope. These teach them a practical skill if they had to sneak away from an assailant, crawl under a truck or other object for cover from someone or simply crawl down a smoke-filled hallway in a burning building. If they get used to crawling in practice then they will not be so disoriented by the idea that they might need to do so in real life.

Below is a drill consisting of ground sidekicks. The student does a sidekick then switches hands and turns the body to the other side to execute a sidekick with the opposite leg. This is continued back and forth.

Ground sidekicks

Rather than only doing various types of sit-ups, I have students do punch sit-ups. They either rise up and fire two-punches straight ahead, or they rise up and fire a right punch to the left and a left punch to the right. The idea is that the student is ready and able and trained to be prepared to fight from any position. Doing workout drills with more of a martial flair to them gives the drills more significance than simply say that sit-ups are to build strong abdominal muscles and nothing else.

Often when students are doing the "crawl for life" we will have instructors or other students hitting them with padded bats and throwing various relatively safe objects at them such as training pads. This creates a more distracting and hostile environment while they are trying to crawl, keep their head down and now keep their head covered to protect it from injuries by objects or assailants.

Punch sit-ups

Many of these drills are classroom versions of military obstacle courses and are intended to serve the same purpose; to prepare the student for combat and for unpleasant situations. These few examples give you the idea of how traditional calisthenics are replaced with similar exercises with the same physical benefits, but with an added component of practical survival skill building built in.

Practice

In all things, when trying to develop a new skill or technique, practice it, learn the correct way to do it, but do not try too hard to make it work. If you are trying too hard, it will not happen. Only when you have let go and leave it alone for a while can something difficult become easy or possible. This applies to many things.

Practice does not make perfect. You might practice all day long, but if you are practicing the wrong way, you are merely emphasizing the wrong way of doing whatever you are practicing. Learn the correct way to practice what you are working on and then practice it perfectly.

As a martial artist, you have many different skills to acquire. It is not possible to possible to practice each of them in a given workout or training session. You must work on some new material and some older material so that you do not lose critical skills that you have acquired.

Techniques and Development

When you are comfortable with certain techniques, stop using them for a while and work to become comfortable with several others. This change of focus helps build your repertoire.

- - - - - - - - - -

When training, work on what does not come naturally until it becomes natural, then work on something new. It does not develop your skill to spend time on techniques that you have mastered. Remember the techniques that you have mastered were once unnatural and required practice.

Never be comfortable with where you are. There is always more skill or knowledge to acquire. If you think there is no more knowledge or skill to acquire, then reflect on this. Study others and you will see that you have much that you can learn and do. There is no end to it.

Stretching

No matter what the body type, stretching is important and beneficial. Stretching helps reduce injuries, increase speed of motion, range of motion, general mobility and improve coordination.

There are two types of stretching: stretching to increase flexibility and stretching to increase mobility. When beginning a workout I have students loosen up very lightly before starting so that they can carefully work out any muscle and joint stiffness that they may have when they come into the dojo. It is critical for students to loosen up before exercising. Stretching helps increase mobility of muscles and joints in preparation for the exercises, drills and other workout content to which students will be subjected. You should do incremental stretching throughout the workout or training session.

Joints and muscles that are more fluid are not as susceptible to injury and can help the martial artist with increased speed in his techniques. This benefit is both physical and psychological. For example, I know that when certain muscles or joints are tight or stiff, I will not move as quickly and I will have a conscious aversion to moving a joint or muscle as quickly as I know that I could otherwise, simply because I am aware of the reduced mobility and the possibility that it will cause damage.

The improved coordination of flexible muscles and joints comes from the greater control and fluidity that result from effective stretching. Muscles and joints that are more fluid and mobile are easier to control and allow the martial artist to more easily practice drills that aid in coordination and agility. Improved speed comes from having generally looser joints and muscles so that reactions and direct actions can be carried out without the negative resistance caused by less resilient muscles and joints. Flexibility also aids in a greater balance among the various muscles and more fluid, less choppy, wasteful movement and conservation of energy.

Injuries and Healing

In a real fight, try not to ever let your opponent see that you are injured. Play off your injury if possible. Even if your injury is visible or noticeable, let your opponent think that it is not affecting you. This will make him stop and think that maybe his techniques are ineffective. In other situations, depending upon the opponent and the circumstances you may want to pretend that you are injured worse than you are – remember the strategies of opposites. Pretending a more serious injury can give your opponent a false sense of security thinking that he is close to defeating you. Then you will have him. This is deception at its best.

It also helps not to focus on you. Keep your eyes and your mind on your opponent in a real fight. Injuries can be dealt with later; a real opponent must be dealt with immediately.

If you are training and you receive an injury, tend to it immediately. Prolonging the treatment could make it worse. Do not make a big deal of the injury every time or you will be easily distracted in a real fight. Learn to be able to tell what is serious and what is minor.

Do not train with injuries that could worsen by training. Allow the injury time to heal completely, and then slowly work back into your routine with caution.

First Aid and Emergency Medicine

Martial arts techniques are generally intended to cause damage to an opponent. You may accidentally cause this damage to your training partner or you may become injured in practice or on the street. In either case knowledge of first aid, CPR, and the basics of how to handle different types of medical emergencies is essential for the martial artist or anyone interested in survival.

In the old days, many martial artists were also doctors or men of medicine. This was because they or their students suffered occasional injuries and there was not always a doctor available, so they had to learn whatever they could to help themselves through an injury or accident. The knowledge of how to heal is just as important as the knowledge of how to damage.

In urban combat or open warfare, first aid training must include proper knowledge of how to respond to and address the following types of injuries and scenarios:

- Major and minor cuts and bleeding
- Joint sprains
- Broken arms, legs, ribs, fingers, toes
- Head injuries: concussion, fractured skull
- Eye injuries
- Fever and infection
- Shock
- Hypothermia
- Heat stroke
- Heat exhaustion
- Heart attack
- Poisonous insect and snake bits
- Poisonous plants
- Burns
- Falls
- Nosebleeds
- Sunburn
- Animal bites
- Tick bites

In your first aid kit, you should consider carrying the following items. This is a fairly advanced and robust kit for serious injuries and emergencies. Take formal first aid training and consider emergency medical technician (EMT) or medic training depending upon your needs. Study the proper use of all contents of the first aid or trauma kit and practice their use frequently. Never administer first aid or medical assistance for which you have not been properly trained and certified.

First Aid/EMT Supplies & Equipment		
2x2" gauze pads	Ibuprofen	anti-itch cream
4x4" gauze pads	Acetaminophen	antacid tablets
5x9" large gauze trauma pads	insect sting ointment	antihistamines
Ace bandage 2" wide and 4" wide	Triple antibiotic	EMT shears
2x2" gauze pads	LED flashlight	pocket knife
4x4" gauze pads	Ibuprofen	first aid guide
4x8" large gauze trauma pads	insect sting ointment	tweezers
assorted band aids	triple antibiotic	chemical glo-sticks
Ace bandage 2" wide	sunscreen SPF 30	burn gel
white medical tape	Sam splints	anti-diarrhea medicine such as pink bismuth
suture kit	smelling salts	decongestant
medical instruments kit (hemostats, scalpels, retractors)	electrolyte tablets	aloe-vera gel
medical instruments kit (hemostats, scalpels)	Aspirin	thermometer
cotton swabs	moleskin	tongue depressor
alcohol gel hand sanitizer	Povodine-Iodine prep pads	alcohol wipes
2" gauze rolls	Sawyer extractor kit	lighter
4" gauze rolls	saline solution eyewash	
mouth barrier	stethoscope	
hydrogen peroxide	triangular bandage	

Limits

Everything and everyone has limits. Know what they are. This may be the limit of someone's patience or your own. You need to know the limit or length of your kicks. You need to know your physical limits of endurance or strength.

Make a note and pay attention to your physical and mental limits. If you know that you cannot lift a certain weight or run a certain distance, then do not do it. If you have a current limit, you can however, gradually, slowly and with care, extend this limit. Begin sparring for one minute. Do this for as long as it takes until one minute is no longer a challenge or a benefit, then increase to one and a half minutes and so on until you are working for good lengths of time.

Know your mental limits as well. If you cannot develop strategy or clearly understand techniques, then consider what weakness you may need to address that will increase your understanding or make it possible for you to develop the strategy that you would like.

Back up from it and take one piece at a time, this makes everything easier. Once you reassemble all of the pieces, you will be able to define your limit and extend it because you understand why it is a limit and why it is holding you back.

Frustration

Why do you get frustrated? If you understood what caused you to be frustrated in your training, maybe you would not be frustrated. Frustration also stems from either not knowing your limits or simply not being willing or patient enough with yourself to accept your current limits and work within them.

Frustration can be an obstacle or deterrent or a temporary roadblock to further progress. Frustration is an emotion that masks another problem. It prevents progress and learning. Therefore, it is important to understand the kinds of things that can cause frustration so that you may address them.

You may become frustrated when your instructor explains something; you try it and you are not successful because you did not understand the explanation. If you failed to understand the explanation, that is the instructor's fault, not yours. Ask your instructor to explain it until you understand better what you are attempting to learn. This frustration can be a lack of physical preparation to engage adequately in a new challenge. Ask your instructor or ask yourself what you should do to prepare better physically or mentally for a new challenge. Once you have addressed this, then you can proceed with the lesson, better equipped for success.

You may be frustrated by the complexity of something new that you are learning. If it is too complex to take in at once, break it down into manageable steps. This is so simple, but very few people practice this.

You cannot become a black belt or a highly skilled martial artist overnight. Everyone knows this. You must build your black belt skill and knowledge over years of carefully structured learning and training. The finished product is the end of a construction project using basic building blocks.

You must approach anything new, difficult or challenging by dividing it. You have heard the saying divide and conquer. Why take on the entirety of a problem, when you can solve it in pieces. Try it. This will remove much frustration. You will see that nearly anything is doable if broken down into small enough pieces. There is no secret here, only work, willingness and persistence.

Visualization

Coaches, trainers and martial artists will agree that visualization is essential in accomplishing goals or developing skill. If you want to become better at a given technique or learn to defeat a certain move that another martial artist has perfected, you must learn to visualize this.

Picture yourself in slow motion defending against the move and try out different responses in slow motion. When you have a response that will counter or defeat the move then replay this vision in your head until you see it in real-time. Then begin to practice this defense on your own or with a partner.

Visualization programs the mind to lead the body.

As you practice, you will have the vision in your mind of what you must do. At that point, all you are really doing is matching your movements to the vision in your mind. When your opponent throws his favorite move, you will have an appropriate response. Time it well.

Wilderness Survival

Many warriors such as Samurai and Hwa Rang studied various aspects of wilderness survival. A fully prepared and well-trained martial artist is concerned with survival from many perspectives. Survival may be in a parking lot or in the wilderness. Any well-rounded martial artist should become skilled in the art of wilderness survival. Wilderness survival generally comes in two modes, one is where you have nothing to work with but your skill and knowledge because you have no supplies, tools or survival equipment; the other is where you are adequately equipped with some basic survival supplies and equipment which makes your situation more manageable and comfortable. You need to have skill and knowledge to succeed in either scenario.

Learn what the appropriate survival items would be to have on hand. In a survival situation, your goals are essentially as follows:

First Aid: Tend to small cuts and injuries so that they do not become infected which can dramatically worsen your situation. Stick to trails or safe terrain to minimize the chances of incurring additional injuries. Know first aid for a variety of injuries.

Shelter: You need protection from the elements, heat or cold – to prevent your core body temperature from becoming too low or too high. There are simple ways to build a basic shelter. A shelter can be built out of a space blanket to protect from the rain. A shelter can be made of a heavy branch against a tree at an angle, covered with a lattice work of smaller branches and as much as two to three feet of leaves for warmth in the winter or just a thin layer of pine boughs or dry leaves to protect from rain and wind in the summer.

Water: You can live for a long while without food, but lack of water and dehydration can kill you in a short time. Typically, a person can live for about three days without water; however, in hotter climates you will need more water to stay sufficiently hydrated. You must be familiar with one or more methods of purifying water. Four methods of purification are boiling, filtering, distilling and chemical treatment. Distilling results in the most pure water. If you cannot distill water with a solar still or over a fire, you can use one of the other methods or combine them such as combining a filter with water purification tablets.

Fire: You will need to stay warm and have the ability to stave off hypothermia. If you get wet even in temperatures in the fifties or low sixties you could be in serious trouble. Always have three methods with you to start a fire, but if you don't know a couple of methods to start a fire with friction and practice them occasionally so that you are confident in your ability. You need to carry some type of fire starter material or tinder. My favorite is a small plastic bag with about eight cotton balls covered with petroleum jelly. These are lightweight; burn even when wet and a single cotton ball is enough to start a fire and will burn for approximately eight minutes.

Food: If you can identify edible plants, or set snares and traps for small game such as rabbits, squirrels, etc, you will be able to cook these over your fire if you have not prepared ahead of time with some basic survival foods.

Signaling: If you are in an area where there is the possibility of being spotted or rescued, stay put and develop some means of signaling. Build a fire that generates smoke in the daytime or light at night. Use a signal mirror effectively, or have a three-foot square of bright orange cloth or safety vest that you can wave or lay on the ground in a clearing in the woods for visibility from the air, or use a whistle to signal nearby searchers. Have a signal fire ready to light in the event an aircraft or ship passes by. Damp foliage will produce large amounts of smoke to improve your visibility.

Learn these skills and practice them often. One never knows when it might come in handy and literally make the difference between life and death. Too many people are completely unprepared for even the most basic emergencies.

Survival Essentials: These are commonly known as outdoor essentials. These essentials are something that should be stored in a small daypack in your car or carried with you in a compact form anywhere in the field. The list includes:

- Extra bright LED Flashlight (with extra batteries)
- Compass and map of the region
- Whistle – for signaling
- Pocket knife or multi-tool (good quality not cheap)
- Three methods of starting a fire (waterproof matches, flint and steel, lighter)
- Fire starter material (cotton balls covered in petroleum jelly)
- Trail mix and power bars
- Extra water

- Extra clothes to provide layers of warmth
- First Aid Kit
- Signal mirror
- Rain gear
- Space blanket – for warmth, shade or rain cover
- Emergency space sleeping bag
- Water purification tablets (military water purification tablets are especially effective because they treat turbidity, which can harbor additional bacteria or viruses that normal purification tablets will not treat.)

Additional Useful Items:
- 50' length of rope
- Pocket survival guide or laminated survival cards
- Emergency fishing kit stored in a small tin
- Three-foot square of bright orange material for signaling to the air or to a ship
- Leather work gloves
- Wide-brimmed hat
- Bandana
- 6 Tea bags
- 6 Instant coffee packets/sticks
- Poncho
- Lip balm with sunscreen
- Sunscreen
- 4 Hot Cocoa packets
- 4 Soup packets
- Small flat roll duct tape
- 8 nails
- 8 Powdered energy drink packets/sticks with electrolytes
- Pocket stove with fuel tabs (small twigs can be used for fire if you run out of fuel tabs)
- Military canteen cup for drinking or eating and heating water
- Chemical heat packs such as the ones hunters use to warm hands and feet and for treating hypothermia
- Tarp for shelter

As you train and practice in wilderness survival you will find that you may have different equipment needs and survival priorities according to where you are located. Survival techniques in a dessert climate are clearly different from those required in an arctic climate. Learn what is appropriate for forest, desert, arctic, mountainous or jungle climates and terrain.

Sharing Knowledge: Teaching

Knowledge, experience and skill serve two purposes, you can use them and you can transmit them to those who are interested in learning. You as a martial artist should be secure in your station. You should not be afraid to give or receive knowledge. Receiving will make you more knowledgeable, giving knowledge will help you understand what you know.

The arts of open-handed combat, self-defense, weapons, development of the character, mind, body and spirit must be passed on to the next generation for their benefit. This happens through teaching and sharing.

All that you will gain and experience must be shared or it will be lost. Teaching gives the arts a sense of immortality. As long as they are passed on they have a chance to live. If they are not, they will surely die out.

Martial Arts Organizations

There are many martial arts clubs, associations and organizations in existence today. Many of these organizations function as the caretakers of their various styles and keep close watch over the teaching of these styles and the standards of performance and advancement.

It is important for students to understand the importance and the role that these organizations play in the martial arts world. To understand better the structure and role of these organizations it is useful to step back for a moment and consider the evolution of martial arts systems.

From the first time that primitive man discovered that he could stick his foot out and trip an adversary, fighting and martial techniques have evolved. The martial systems that we study today are largely derived from systems that were developed by individuals. These individuals developed systems of self-defense, gave them names, refined them and began to teach them to others. Students of these instructors were the proving ground for these martial systems and the masters continued to refine, innovate and evolve their systems and styles. As the systems developed into maturity, various ranking schemes evolved with most of them. Students were identified by their rank and instructors could gauge their ability even without personally knowing the student. As more curriculum came into being, higher ranks were possible. Students who stayed with a master for a long enough time could rise in rank and skill as the master's own skill expanded and the curriculum with it.

Various systems adopted sophisticated philosophical and spiritual bases upon which they built their techniques, strategies and customs. Like any family tree, the martial arts family tree has many branches in many countries. Each time a senior instructor would leave a master, he would go to another location, teach what he had learned and in many cases modify, innovate and adapt his original system into a variant of what he had mastered. In some cases, major innovations came into existence by the hard work, analysis and creative insight of masters who devised systems that were significantly different from what they had originally learned.

Morehei Ueshiba, the founder of Aikido (meaning "Harmony Way") built his system based on the philosophy that he respected his opponent and therefore wished no harm to his adversary. The original techniques that he developed caused no permanent harm to the adversary. There were no strikes or kicks that would inflict damage that would prevent an opponent from recovering after a time and coming back to continue an assault. I believe that philosophy, although honorable, is not a practical basis for a robust system of self-defense. Opponents will get up and return to the fight, at least until the defender has shown through enough attempts that he is impervious. Conversely, the general strategy in Kenpo Karate is to cause maximum damage in a complete flurry of devastating techniques. These styles of martial arts are on opposite ends of the force continuum.

Later variations of Aikido began to incorporate some number of simple kicks and strikes for use on a limited basis for persistent attackers. Later students of Ueshiba and his son developed these variations and they are now part of the martial family tree.

Tae Kwon Do and all of the other major and minor systems of martial arts have evolved, branched and morphed into a myriad of flavors all having some common elements. It is part of the martial tradition for a senior student to leave his master, go on his own, reflect and adapt and hopefully devise some useful innovations or potentially even introduce a radically new style or system. This keeps the arts dynamic, vibrant and growing.

In modern times, along with the development of new styles and systems comes the evolution of martial arts organizations and associations. These organizations charge membership and testing fees and provide some degree of quality assurance over their domain. Students derive a sense of legitimacy by receiving black belt certifications. Aside from revenue generation for the leaders of the organizations, certification and rank testing are usually promoted as providing acceptance for the students. If you obtain a black belt from organization "A", then you will be recognized anywhere that organization has a school or club. The problem with the recognition or certification is that many organizations refuse to recognize each other. These organizations typically require students to re-test on material that is very similar.

Often one organization may look upon black belts from another similar organization as being illegitimate. There are politics and egos involved and many organizations have come into being simply because the leadership of one organization had a falling out or fundamental differences so a divergence occurred and several new organizations then came into existence.

Another inconvenient feature of the organizations is that they periodically make subtle changes in the curriculum and the expected way in which the students are to perform the material. This is solely for requiring instructors to attend teaching seminars and to act as a control mechanism so that the organization maintains control over its affiliate schools. There are no practical, martial reasons for example, in changing how many Kihaps (yells) there are in a pattern, or on which moves they are to occur. This keeps instructors and students on their toes with useless and frivolous changes where time could be better spent focusing on the Bunkai (practical application), which most organizations do not teach.

What are the advantages of these modern martial arts organizations? There is robust curriculum; however, lacking it may be in specific focus on self-defense. These organizations are prevalent, instruction is usually consistent, and instructors do receive thorough training, which improves the student's experience. However, these martial organizations are highly politically charged often with much in-fighting. Self-defense and street survivability is often covered as more of an afterthought or an adjunct to the traditional curriculum, whereas if the focus were on the interpretation of the kata (Bunkai), then students would be learning what the movements of the patterns could do rather than learning to mimic a specific performance for purposes of passing a belt test. I have seen master-level classes where self-defense is not even discussed except in academic terms, not because there is any practical consideration of the need for it. The result, I believe, is students who are highly trained and tested in the tradition, etiquette, symbolic meanings and history of the kata and proper performance of techniques, but uneducated in the adaptation of these techniques and practical application for survival.

* * *

Take two or three of the concepts in this chapter and practice them during a given workout. Use techniques from your style of martial art to apply the concepts. Practice these concepts and drills for about five workouts until you have become comfortable and developed some noticeably improved proficiency. It is an experiment to see how these concepts work and feel. When you have finished with this series of workouts where you have applied two or three of these concepts in various drills, then take some notes in your martial arts notebook. Write down what you learned; the types of drills you did and what you gained from them. Then for your next five workouts, pick two more of the concepts in this chapter and apply them. Take notes after you have completed those workouts and continue through this chapter and the next one applying the concepts. I recommend you try these concepts in the order they are presented. For the most part they build on each other. As you progress through this chapter and incorporate these guidelines into your training, you will be growing significantly in your understanding of training and the skills you are developing.

Chapter 3

Strategy and Tactics

Training the Mind

"Let what works well be the test for what is right."

Bruce Lee

Strategy is the knowledge of how to combine and use techniques and tactics effectively. Strategy is the means by which you defeat your opponent or stay alive. Strategy develops the mind of the martial artist. Technique and skill alone cannot ensure victory. To pursue your goals in life you will need to build upon your skills and develop a framework or menu of useful strategies in which to employ these skills to take you to your objectives.

Strategy is your approach to accomplishing your goals in the encounter. To have a strategy, you must first establish your goals. A strategy without goals is void, there is no such thing. This applies to all things.

Also, remember that the beginner cannot be concerned with strategy. It is too advanced; they are concerned merely with standing up and trying to execute appropriate techniques. Strategy is many levels above the beginner. Beginners should be concerned with techniques and technical proficiency. A martial artist must first develop technical proficiency like learning how to read and write well, before he can attempt to develop or study strategy. When a student can execute a wide variety of techniques with grace, control and proficiency then they can begin to think about and incorporate concepts of simple strategies.

- - - - - - - - - -

As the student develops skill in strategy he will see that every move, every feint, every shift of weight serves a purpose and can be used as part of some strategy. Ultimately, strategy gives purpose to all movement and thought. This is the level of realization to strive for with strategy development.

Theory

Bruce Lee said, "Take what is useful from all styles and make it work for you. Do not be bound by a single system of martial arts, but learn to appreciate all systems." His book, The Tao of Jeet Kune Do, the way of the intercepting fist is not a book about a particular style because he said that Jeet Kune Do is not a style, but a philosophy toward studying the martial arts techniques strategies and tactics. My book is about understanding what topics a martial artist should study, how to study them, how they relate to each other and the meanings of key concepts. Bruce Lee takes these concepts further into the technical realm and analyzes them to determine the proper and optimum application of concepts and techniques. You must study theory, understand it and apply it in practice and in reality.

The Strategies of Opposites

Opposites are key concepts in the understanding and consideration of strategy, training and martial arts. They are valuable keys to recognizing what is appropriate and when. Opposites are simple, yet powerful strategies. Consider these examples carefully and develop more of your own:

- - - - - - - - - -

When your opponent is strong, make him think that you are weak. They will be overconfident about your weakness and their strength and then you can win.

- - - - - - - - - -

When your opponent is weak, show him that you are strong. He will cower in the shadow of your strength and you can win.

- - - - - - - - - -

If your opponent fights fast and moves fast, then move slowly. He will expect you to keep up with him, do not. Then he will be wary and frustrated. While he is fast and you are slow, you can watch his movement more easily as he goes by and know when and where to strike because you are not busy trying to keep up.

- - - - - - - - - -

When your opponent is slow and cautious, be confident and swift. Overwhelm his cautiousness. Force him to react when he is not prepared. He will become frustrated and lose control, and then you can win.

- - - - - - - - - -

Do not always be the opposite of your opponent. He may expect this. Mimic your opponent. Do what he does. He will notice this and be angry or distracted, feeling that he is fighting himself. Then surprise him when he notices that you are copying him. Then you have him.

- - - - - - - - - -

When you are near your opponent make him feel like you are far away and out of reach.

- - - - - - - - - -

When you are far away and safe, make your opponent think you are within reach. This is frustrating to him. Think about how to apply this.

- - - - - - - - - -

Sun Tzu said, "Deception is the key to victory in all warfare."

Deceive your enemy with opposites. Make him always think that things are different from what they really are. This applies to many things. Vary your strategy of opposites and consciously cycle through several of the previous strategies to force your opponent to adjust to your strategies and tactics. If your tactics are changing frequently then it will be difficult to keep pace with what you are doing and that will give you an advantage.

- - - - - - - - - -

When you are strong and fit, pretend that you are injured and weak.

- - - - - - - - - -

When you are weak or tired, do not let it show or you opponent will move in.

- - - - - - - - - -

When your opponent tries to crowd you and stay close, keep him away.

- - - - - - - - - -

When your opponent tries to keep his distance from you, crowd him, make him nervous and uncomfortable. He will be thinking of getting away, and then you will have him.

- - - - - - - - - -

When on the defensive, make it look like you are attacking.

- - - - - - - - - -

When you are in the midst of an attack, make your opponent think that you are on the defensive and not actually going all out.

- - - - - - - - - -

When you opponent is hard and forceful, be soft and yielding. Use his force and power against him and re-direct it toward him. Do the opposite as well.

- - - - - - - - - -

When running away or retreating, make your opponent think that you are attacking and vice-versa.

After you have practiced and incorporated these types of strategies into your workouts and training you will be ready to expand beyond them and develop or innovate your own strategies of opposites. Think about what strategies of opposites you could add to the ones above.

Thinking

There should be little or no thinking when fighting for real. You should be thinking during training to learn and become knowledgeable of technique and approaches. However, in a real situation, your perceptions must become your actions and this will protect you.

Real situations do not allow time for thought, so do not depend upon conscious selection for your response to a technique, but rely on subconscious reactions. This is your best protection. Use conscious thought for developing and adjusting strategy. If you have trained well and your training has become subconscious, then you will be well off.

Techniques and tactics should be subconscious and require almost no thought. Consciously rotate from one strategy to another to keep your opponent on guard. Once you have practiced many strategies, like techniques, you will be able to almost instantly select a strategy and use it for a time until you decide to adjust and change to another strategy and set of tactics. There is no real thinking or planning going on here. It is a matter of choosing from a menu that you have already established during your training.

As I have said, a thinking fighter with good technical skill is difficult to defeat. When two martial artists are both good thinkers, then victory will belong to the one who is better conditioned and has superior technical ability. If two martial artists have equal technical ability, then victory will belong to the one with higher intelligence, greater creativity and greater skill at deception.

- - - - - - - - - -

When sparring with an opponent, always try to think of the big picture. Do not play checkers, just one move at a time in a purely reactionary mode. To gain the advantage you must shift from reactionary mode to proactive mode so that you begin to take control of the situation with the strategy you have chosen. Pick your strategy and the moves will help you accomplish your strategy as if picking a la cart from a menu. Visualize several moves ahead like in chess. This takes practice during your training, but then in a real situation it will happen almost subconsciously if you have practiced effectively.

- - - - - - - - - -

Remember the things in this book require thought. You will have to read and re-read these passages many times because you will have developed a better understanding each time you consider these concepts. If they seem difficult at first, do not be concerned. Practice these ideas. Thinking is for the mind as training is for the body. If you have the patience or determination to train and develop your body, you should also apply this diligence to training your mind. However, like a body, not everyone's mind may be as fit or capable, but you can still improve it beyond where it is now.

Self-Defense

In the past, self-defense allowed an individual to use any technique or means of escape or damage to neutralize a threat from an opponent. In recent times, many assailants have used the legal system to fight back against the very individuals they sought to rob or injure.

In the past, you could use self-defense to cause maximum damage if so desired. Today, you must use self-defense or martial arts techniques to cause minimal damage, except in truly life threatening situations. Self-defense techniques today emphasize what I call the soft-style, non-destructive, approach. Self-defense of the past relied on more hard-style, destructive techniques. It is useful to practice both. These hard and soft techniques span the force continuum.

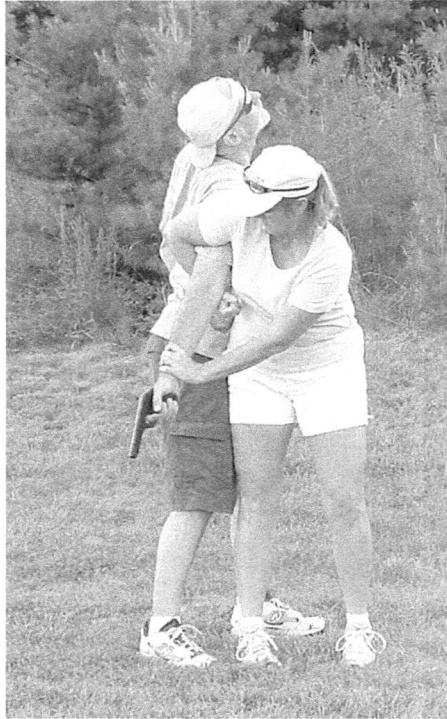

Whenever possible, hide your movement and disguise it well. Make the damaging techniques look accidental. Do not make it obvious that you are a martial artist. Being a martial artist carries a large degree of liability in such cases, because we are supposed to know better than to destroy our opponent even if we have been violated physically.

The martial artist who uses destructive techniques today may be in a vulnerable position, not in the alley, but later, in the courtroom. Unfortunately, this is the nature of things today. The only viable approach to self-defense is to give your opponent the benefit of the doubt, cause little or no permanent harm or injury to him physically or he may cause financial and legal harm to you later. Nonetheless, you have the right to defend yourself and if you truly feel that your safety is in danger then employ whatever you judge to be appropriate force in response. Pacifists become statistics.

Recycling

Do not allow an opponent to use a weapon (gun/knife/arm/leg) again after you have disarmed them. Stepping on the weapon, tossing, or kicking it away prevents recycling.

However, you do want to recycle your own weapons and reuse them as often as is appropriate – circular strikes (vertical or horizontal) can be easily repeated, modified and used repeatedly and combined with hip rotation for added power.

If you grab an arm or wrist or foot – do not let go. These are weapons. If you have one, damage it or control it so that your opponent cannot use it against you again.

Attacking the Weapon

Punch the arm or block the arm that is punching to hurt the arm or wrist. Hurt the knee, foot, or leg so that it cannot be used to kick again. If the situation is serious, break the wrist, shoulder, elbow, or fingers so that they cannot be used again to hurt you! You must decide what is appropriate.

The defender, in white, blocks the punching arm and grabs it at the same time while striking the weapon with a perpendicular hard block as he steps off the line of attack.

Natural Vulnerabilities

There are many natural vulnerabilities in the human body. There is a front, centerline and a rear centerline. The diagrams below show the targets on the front and rear of the body. Attack the nose, throat, groin, eyes, ears, spine, knees, ankles, wrists, fingers, elbows, back of neck.

Eyes
Temple
Jaw
Throat
Elbow
Groin
Inner thigh femoral artery
Bridge of foot

Ears
Carotid arteries
Chin "button"
Solar plexus
Side of knee
Shin
Ankle

Targets on the front of the body

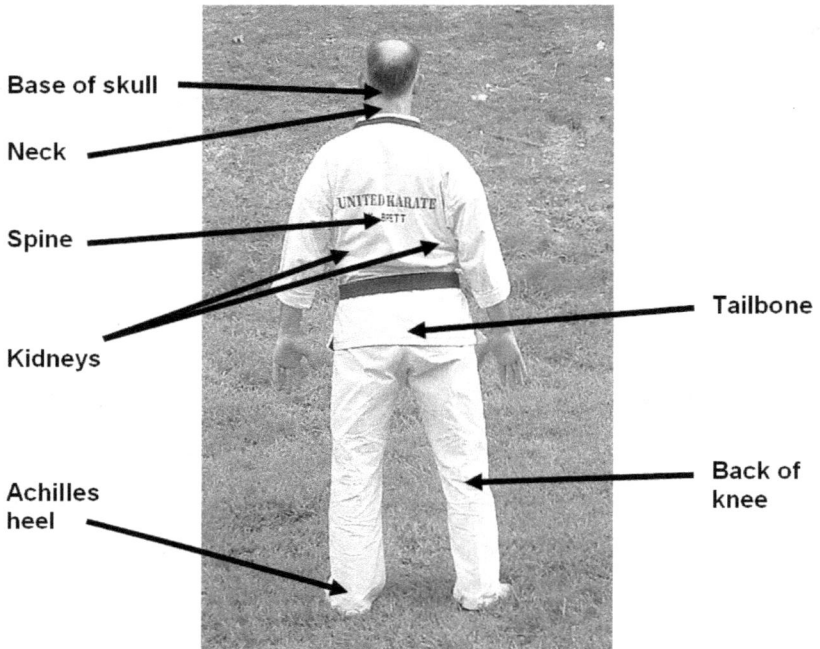

Base of skull

Neck

Spine

Kidneys

Tailbone

Achilles heel

Back of knee

Targets on the back of the body

Decisiveness

Do not hesitate. Wait, be prepared, time your technique and strike, but do not hesitate. Take the advantage before your opponent seizes it. Decisiveness is essential in survival situations so that you may pre-empt your opponent. Pre-emption is necessary when you sense or read your opponent and determine that they are about to strike or position themselves in some way that increases the threat they pose to you. Be decisive on a course of action to prevent your opponent from realizing his plans.

Distraction

Distraction is not the same as faking. When you fake, you make your opponent think one thing is happening when it is not.

Distraction gives your opponent something to focus on or deal with while you follow up with your true intentions. The idea is that by the time you follow up with your true intentions, your opponent is still too busy dealing with what preceded them.

The difference between a distraction and a fake is that with a distraction you actually are doing something; with a fake, you are only making your opponent think that you are doing something. This applies to combat, self-defense and many things.

Distractions are not necessarily always physical movements. They may be psychological also. You may distract an attacker who is intent upon doing you harm by talking to him. You may use psychology to distract him and engage him in a conversation, which is actually buying you time to size up the situation better or to maneuver to a more advantageous position.

If you are able to engage your opponent's mind and distract him that way, then you may not have to rely upon physical skill and posturing. Consider the possibilities. This is how hostage negotiators prevent unwanted physical harm from occurring.

Fakes

Fakes must look real or they will not work. A bad fake is worse than no fake because you leave yourself vulnerable. The advantage of a believable fake is that if the opponent does not react in time you may just use the fake for real. To make a fake look real, you must believe that you are actually going to do whatever it is. Then at the last instant, do not do it, pull the technique short and instantly follow it up with the technique you really intended. The purpose of a fake is to make your opponent react to it, generally to create an opening that you can take advantage of with a different technique. For example, a fake kick toward the head might make your opponent raise both arms to guard their face and head. This exposes their torso where you may actually be planning to land a punch.

Make a list of different techniques that you might use for fakes and beside each one indicate what the natural reaction of the opponent would be, what the exposed target might be and which technique you might switch to for the actual follow up to the fake. This way you will have built your own menu of fakes and be able to practice them frequently to maintain a repertoire of effective combinations. However, always remember that whatever technique you choose to fake, the two key elements of an effective fake are that the fake technique must look completely real – especially against an experienced martial artist – and the follow up after the fake must be fast and decisive in order to take advantage of the opening or opportunity that you have created.

Deception

Sun Tzu said that deception is the key to victory in all warfare, but what is deception? If I am to apply it, I must know what it is and how to apply it. What constitutes deception?

Creativity is the key to deception. Think of ways to draw your opponent off their guard. When they are expecting one thing, give them something else. Draw their attention away from your true intentions so that when your true intentions are realized, your opponent will be caught unprepared and surprised. Do not be predictable.

The components of deception are these:
* Creativity
* Feinting or Faking

- Distraction
- Opposites

These components combined intelligently give you the basis of a strategy. I have already told you about distraction, feinting, faking, opposites, and other strategies. You must practice your creativity. Creativity means developing new and different ways of feinting and methods of distraction or the use of opposites.

You must always create or switch to new means of deception because once your opponent recognizes a deceptive tactic, no matter how elusive or cunning, he will be better prepared to counter it. Always give him something new to deal with. This will give you the advantage.

The elements of deception combine to give you the beginnings of a strategy, but they alone are not a strategy. To have a complete strategy you must combine your tactics of deception with a purpose of your intentions. What are you trying to accomplish? When you have a clear vision of what you are trying to accomplish overall, then the tactics and techniques to use in your strategy of deception will be easier to determine.

Hiding Your Motion

A novice or intermediate student or opponent is easy to defeat with reasonably good technique. An advanced student is better at recognizing many techniques and countering them. For this opponent it will be necessary to hide your motion.

This can be done in two ways: either precede your intended technique with a fake, or the more advanced way of hiding motion would be to use a deception where you are not faking, but leading with single or multiple techniques and simultaneously executing your intended technique. For example, a jab to the face may hide a simultaneous sweep or kick to the lead leg. The position or location of your arm, leg or body may actually block your opponent's view of your technique.

Simultaneous punch toward the face, hides the real technique which is the kick to the leg to set up a take down. The punch is then turned into a collar grab to pull the opponent, in black, backward against the direction of the leg kick.

Probing Your Opponent

Whether your opponent is an army of one-hundred-thousand men or a single man, you must probe to find weaknesses and collect information about your opponent's strength, position, mobility, reactions and skill.

Attack your enemy where they are weak, but first know this by probing. Test for weaknesses. Watch closely and observe potential weakness, signs of inexperience or disorganization. If you feint an attack and your enemy does not respond in a way that is adequate for his own defense, then you have discovered a potential weakness or area where you may be able to make an opening.

When you probe your opponent in a particular way, not only make a note of what their response was, but how fast, precise and strong their response was. These factors will be important in determining how to attack and how to construct and time your attack.

- - - - - - - - - -

Another purpose of probing is not just to determine weaknesses in your opponent, but also to determine how they will respond. If you throw a particular technique and they respond in a particular way, they will generally respond this way all of the time.

Your objective here is to remember how they responded. Make a mental note. Then continue probing them in different ways and noting how they respond each time.

When you have noted their responses and you have a sense of how effective or ineffective each response is, then you have a better idea of where to attack, and how.

Probing is the deceptive way of asking your opponent to show you what they are capable of doing. Once they have shown you, you can defeat them if your attacks and strategies are superior and take advantage of your opponent's weaknesses.

Innovation

A martial artist is an artist. The essence of art is to express and to contribute to the art form through innovations.

Innovation is the successful result of experimentation. Anyone can try something different. Develop your skills at improving and working towards creating something new and useful . . . this is innovation.

Practice new things in new ways. Try out things and see if they work or do not work. This is the only way that you will really know something.

An instructor can explain or lecture endlessly and you may or may not grasp what he or she is saying, but in a moment of silence and thought, without saying a word, you can try something or discover something that you can use.

If you try something new and it works, keep it. You have just innovated. Write it down and review it later.

Experimentation

Everything that exists now as tradition was once created through innovation and experimentation. Martial artists should always continue to develop the techniques, styles and traditions of the future. However, martial artists must still study tradition in-depth so that they know the ways and techniques that came before them. To omit the study of history and tradition is to be fated to re-discover that which has already been developed.

Do not confuse experimentation with innovation, anyone can experiment and never come up with a single innovation.

Analysis

A real martial artist must develop skill at analysis. Analysis means studying your opponent or yourself.

To analyze something is to break it down into its smallest components. As you break something down, study the structure of it whether it is a single type of kick or an entire system of martial arts.

Look at what you are analyzing from as many perspectives as you can. Try to describe or identify as many qualities and characteristics or attributes of the thing as you can. When you have made yourself familiar with all of the facets and brought all of this to your attention, then it is time to think.

Consider what you might gain from the things that you have discovered or observed. How can you improve upon these things? What makes them useful or useless? Why do these things fit together or interact the way that they do. All of this has meaning to you; it is up to you to determine its meaning.

- - - - - - - - - -

A martial artist must have the ability to think and analyze his opponent. If he does not, then he is only a technician. If he is only a thinker, and does not have the physical skill or experience to attack or defend in the appropriate manner, then he will not be successful even against someone who has only average skill and lesser intelligence.

Attacking

As I have said, attack your opponent's weaknesses. Of course, you must first discover his weaknesses by probing. Once you have found these, attack them relentlessly. Do no attack him when he is strong or ready, hold off on this or you will be wasting effort.

Attacks can take a variety of forms. They may be like pecking away occasionally to annoy your opponent and gradually wear him down. It could be that his biggest weakness is simply endurance or stamina. You may simply float around him pecking occasionally until he cannot continue. Then either finish him off or leave.

An attack can be a short concentrated burst and then it is over. You can use a short burst to distract and disorient your opponent, putting them at a disadvantage, then follow up with the main body of the attack and finish with the grand finale to secure a final victory.

Another critical concept for you to grasp is that in a self-defense situation your survival may depend upon striking first. At the corps of this concept is a philosophy espoused by Bruce Lee. If you feel that an assault or attack is imminent when you find yourself in a perilous situation and you are convinced that your safety or life is in grave danger – strike first. The pre-emptive strike may give you edge you need to survive. On the street and in combat, there are no extra courtesy points for allowing your assailant to throw the first strike.

Evaluating Your Opponent

Your opponent may be a beginner, more advanced or expert. Within these general levels of ability, the fighter may be of a particular style. There is a lot to observe when dealing with a new opponent.

Beginners have no style. However, since they try out many things, they may, by luck exhibit some properties of a more experienced fighter. This can be confusing unless you are experienced enough to recognize the difference. A beginner may vary their techniques and their rhythm, but this is usually purely by chance. They are too inexperienced and inconsistent to do this well for long and they will soon give themselves away with simple mistakes.

Look at the quality of the technique of a beginner. Do their punches and kicks have enough reach to strike you? Are they using close-range techniques from a distance and distance techniques when they are close?

Does the beginner move jerkily, wasting energy? A more experienced fighter knows not to do this. Does the opponent look away or flinch when you feint an attack. An experienced fighter generally will not.

If your opponent is getting winded quickly, he is inexperienced, even an out of shape experienced fighter would know that he will get winded and will be more conservative with his energy, only throwing techniques that are decisive. A beginner will usually flail away endlessly thinking that he is fighting, when all he is doing is burning up his energy. When he runs out of energy, the fight is over.

An experienced fighter who is on his guard and is very steady and consistent with no apparent openings is difficult to attack by simply going at him directly. This type of fighter will stop you when you approach him.

You must be more cunning, draw him towards you, and make him expose his openings. Make him feel secure enough that he will attempt an attack, and then he is exposed.

- - - - - - - - - -

Beginners generally will fall into one of three categories and will often change from one category to another because they are so inconsistent. They are still trying to discover or establish their style of fighting, but do not yet know how.

The first category or mode of beginner is offensive only. These people will attack all the time until they drop from exhaustion. They are overly confident or so scared that they think that if they keep on top of their opponent, they will be in control.

The second category is defensive only. These kinds of fighters are timid and unsure of themselves or simply terrified of their opponent and they will stay covered awaiting the inevitable attack. They are afraid to try any offense.

Thirdly, beginners will be inconsistent, they will be partly offensive, when they think that they have the upper hand and partly defensive when they are unsure of themselves or realize that they are in over their head.

This third type of fighter actually has the best potential to become good. These fighters have at least some sense to know they are outmatched and some sense of knowing when it might be a good time to try some offense. This way they are doing three things that the other two types of fighters are not doing. One, they are trying offense; two, they are trying defense; three, they are thinking a little bit and adapting to the situation. These are critical skills in martial arts and self-defense.

Targets and Weaknesses

Even a strong body has many weaknesses. The way that we humans are constructed and function is truly amazing, but we are not perfect mechanisms.

Every target is a weakness in our structure or function. If it is not a weakness, then it is not a target. Why attack something that is strong. Remember to attack where they are weak.

Learn anatomy well. This will help you to understand what you are doing to your opponent and what is happening to you. Knowledge of anatomy will make weaknesses readily apparent. This will help you understand how to attack your enemy and how to protect yourself.

Appearances

As I have already said, when you are practicing something new, do not try too hard or it will not work. Leave it alone and come back to it with a new perspective.

Appearances are much the same. Do not look at something such as a technique that your opponent uses successfully for too long. Looking at it too long and not making any headway toward defeating the technique or learning your own new techniques could mean that they are not what they appear to be. The difficulties that you may be having may be because the way you see it is not the way that it is.

There are many instances when you may look at a thing that appears to be one way and you assume that it is this way. However, you are not able to make sense of it because something is not clear, something is missing, or it is simply not what it appears to be.

A round kick may, first appear to be a hook kick. A back fist may appear to be a straight punch. A technique or opponent may at first, appear to be fast when in reality they simply have good timing. Remember the strategies of opposites. Make things appear to be one way when they are really another.

Look strong, even when you are weak and beware that a weak-looking or smaller-sized opponent may appear to be less of a threat on appearances than in reality.

Therefore, things that may appear to be one way may actually be something entirely different, which could catch you off guard. Be cautious not to allow yourself to be misled by appearances. There is often more than meets the eye. This is the domain of feints, distractions and deceptions.

Often we make assumptions about the way something is because of the way it appears to be. Question these assumptions. Back away from them and approach your quandary in a different way. You may discover what has eluded you to this point.

Environment as Strategy

The things around you make up your environment. This includes the terrain, the surfaces covering the terrain, objects, artifacts, obstructions, structures and people around you.

Your environment can be used to your advantage. It can also be used to your opponent's advantage. Beware of this. The ways in which environment can be used are many. You may be able to hide or escape from an opponent in the dark or fog. You may be able to use everyday objects around you as weapons to add to your empty-handed defense.

You can use a wall or a railing to push off or as a support for throwing a kick to make you more stable and less vulnerable. You can throw objects in the path or the face of your attacker to distract him and buy you time to maneuver or escape.

You can use nearly any object around you to throw, swing, tip, spray or move rapidly and easily to put time or distance between you and your opponent. Consider the possibilities often and you will be surprised what you find that you had never noticed. However, do not get too caught up in a desperate self-defense situation trying to find too many objects or obstructions that may actually slow you down more than they do your opponent.

Holding on to the side of a vehicle for extra balance when throwing a kick provides an advantage.

Whenever using weapons of opportunity or aspects of your environment they must be readily accessible and useable, only requiring a split second to grab or put to use to aid your defense or to provide some momentary advantage. Anything more will actually put you at a disadvantage.

Terrain as Strategy

You can train, study and prepare, but if when you are in a self-defense situation or any other form of combat, you do not have a grasp of the terrain and its surfaces, then you may be surprised and defeated.

It is essential, as I have said to vary your training. This includes varying the type of terrain or surfaces upon which you train. Your training should give you the opportunity to train on grass, dirt, gravel, in the water or mud and on smooth surfaces such as ice or tiles. All of these surfaces require you to adapt and select different techniques and strategies from your library.

Terrain is not merely the surfaces of the ground upon which you stand, but the contours of the ground beneath these surfaces. As Sun Tzu said, terrain can have many characteristics, which can give the advantage or take away an advantage.

Terrain can provide an escape route such as in wide-open areas. Another escape route may be a wooded area or a maze of alleys where you may give your opponent the slip. You can use terrain as a vantage point, such as at higher elevations. You can use it to encircle or otherwise entrap an opponent. You can use terrain to conceal and protect. This may be good for you or bad for you depending upon whether you are the one concealing yourself or whether your enemy is concealing himself.

Any surface or terrain where your footing or balance is compromised or put at a disadvantage will require you to either grab hold of some handle or railing to stay upright or you will have to lower your center of gravity and your stance to keep from falling.

Use the terrain or objects around you to your advantage. Rocks and boulders offer a shield, concealment or protection. You can kick up loose dirt or throw it in your opponent's face. You may also do this with water or other liquids.

Hiding behind the front or rear of a car while an opponent is at the other end looking for his victim.

If some other surface is so unpredictable or disadvantageous that you cannot maintain balance and control, you may even consider drawing your opponent to the ground and taking the conflict lower, providing that you have trained and studied ground fighting. Then you will have an advantage even on disadvantageous terrain.

You can use icy, snowy surfaces for a ground fight, and then you will not be so concerned with maintaining your balance or footing because you are already down.

If you choose to stay upright, then you must widen your stance to be more flat-footed to maintain traction. Kicks and sweeps are more risky because they reduce your stable base. In these cases, hand techniques may be more appropriate. Your techniques and strategy will vary with the terrain and the surfaces. Find advantages where there appear to be none. This is the essence of victory!

Also, be aware the same advantages you may find, your enemy can use. Do not assume that your opponent will not use the terrain or surfaces to the same advantage that you would.

You must train on different terrains, flat, uneven, hilly, rocks, wooded, cluttered with debris or rubble, in narrow confines such as alleys or elevators, in wide-open places and in streams or inside automobiles or moving trains.

Terrain is a large component of the environment, as I have discussed. The more often you train in different terrains and environments, the more versatile and adaptable you can become.

Creativity

Art is creativity. Creativity is the combination of experimentation, thinking, perception and innovation and sometimes, just luck. The artist's purpose is to express himself. Martial artists express themselves through their techniques, style, choice of weapons, means of training, strategies of self-defense and ways of interacting with and teaching others.

Creativity is a skill like any other. People will tell you that they are either creative or that they are not. Either one may be true, but they do not realize that in either case they can improve their creativity simply by practicing it. The more you do it the easier it is. Practice this in all aspects of martial arts.

Camouflage, Concealment and Evasion

In an emergency survival or combat situation, you may find it necessary to camouflage yourself. Effective camouflage, cover and concealment may allow you to survive versus being captured by an enemy. Camouflage and movement techniques, such as stalking, will also help you track and hunt animals for food using primitive weapons and skills. The essence of camouflage is to transform your appearance to blend in with your surroundings so that you cannot be seen or detected by an enemy.

The three main tactics in camouflage are: to blend with surrounding colors, simulate the texture of your surroundings and breakup the outline of your body so that your shape is not recognized as a human form.

A soldier applies camouflage makeup.

Hiding Your Shape and Outline

Your body will be noticeable because it is a familiar shape. You need to break up your outline by attaching vegetation from the nearby area to your clothing, equipment, and backpack or equipment. Blend in with the surrounding colors and simulate the texture of your surroundings. Once you are camouflaged, there will be times when you need to hide to avoid detection. Cover yourself and your equipment with leaves, grass, or branches, twigs or other local natural materials.

Using Color and Texture

You will have to adjust your camouflage techniques and materials depending upon where you are located. Each geographic area of the world and climatic has unique colors, patterns and textures.

A U.S. Marine sniper is concealed in brush and camouflaged.

Textures vary from rough, to smooth, rocky to leafy. Effective camouflage requires that you use color and texture that matches your surroundings. You may use natural or man-made materials such as camouflage paint, ashes from burned wood or paper, grass, dirt, mud, pine boughs or branches from bushes. You must cover any exposed skin. Use an irregular pattern that appears natural. Areas that protrude and catch more light should be covered with darker colors while areas around the eyes that are more recessed or under the jaw can be covered with lighter colors. As you cover more territory, you will need to take note of changes in your surroundings and specific vegetation and adapt your camouflage accordingly.

If you are in the woods, you need to wear or cover yourself with brush, branches, leaves and other natural materials to blend in. Camouflage can be accomplished using terrain to your advantage. Once you have covered yourself you can blend in to the terrain easily in a well-concealed position.

Covering Shine

Oily skin or equipment that is smooth may shine. This shine will reflect or catch light that may cause you to be detected. Cover shiny objects by smearing them with mud or dirt or give them a light coating of dust or cover them with tape or cloth.

Using Shadows

Shadow can be used for concealment. Stay in the shadow when you move so that light will not catch you. If there is a lot of vegetation, then use this as a visibility barrier between you and your enemy. The more vegetation between you the more difficult it will be to distinguish you from the surrounding vegetation.

In urban areas or where there is a number of man-made structures watch out for where your shadow is cast. Pay attention to the direction of the sun or streetlights at night. You may be hiding behind the corner of a structure, but a light or the sun may cast your shadow beyond the edge of the structure and give away your position. Another hazard to avoid is being in a dark area with a light that is on one side. If there is an enemy in the direction the light is pointing, they will be able to see your silhouette against the light.

Concealing Movement

Ninjas learned to move slowly in order to avoid detection. Fast movement causes noise. When an enemy is nearby, that is the time to remain motionless and silent. Let your camouflage do its job. Fast movement risks detection or injury and burns energy that you may need for long-distance evasion of your enemy.

Go behind obstacles or around them but not over them or you may be exposing yourself. Avoid being on top of a ridge or other high point where your silhouette may give you away. When moving, you must stop occasionally to observe and listen for enemy movement. When you move you can conceal any sound you may make you can take advantage of existing sounds such as strong wind, aircraft, vehicles and other noises to cover the sound of your movement.

Camouflaging Scent

To avoid an enemy you may have to camouflage your scent. An enemy may have dogs or hostile animals in the area may detect your scent and put you at risk. Wash yourself and clothing without soap. Rinse all soap out and body odors. Do not eat or use anything that is sweet smelling or that has any other strong distinctive odor. Use herbs or plants to wash yourself and clothing. Pine needles, leaves or flowers can cover your scent. You can use the smell of a campfire and its smoky scent to give you a less human scent.

Chapter 4

Spirit and Excellence

Training the Soul and Character

"A warrior who has learned the secret to achieving personal excellence must serve as an example and inspiration to others and apply these qualities in all endeavors."

Kevin Brett

Spirit and excellence is the essence of being a martial artist; developing character and attitude, humility, respect, perseverance and an attitude of service to others. Spirit develops the soul and character of the martial artist. To achieve success requires skill and strategy; to maintain that success and build upon it requires a mature character.

- - - - - - - - - -

Ultimately, spirit and excellence make the martial artist. Spirit is not the same as attitude. Attitude is a reflection of spirit. If you have good spirit, it will show in your attitude. Attitude is merely an external manifestation or output of your internal spirit.

A person develops their spirit as they mature. It is a part of their character. If they develop good character and good spirit, then they have the potential to become a good martial artist. If they develop bad character and bad spirit, they will only be capable of learning techniques, not martial arts in the true sense.

Spirit can only be discussed so much. It must be felt, discovered and internalized. Like the opposites of nature, like the Yin and Yang; opposites, which actually contain a part of the other, as you, become a martial artist, martial arts spirit will become a part of you. I hope that you will feel this.

Even if you have read this far, like the continuous motion of the Yin Yang, the subjects in this book are on going. Every time that you read a passage on a subject, you should have a different view about it; more insight than the last time you contemplated it.

Chi

I remember watching "Star Wars", and hearing Obi Wan Kenobi describe "The Force", "It binds us and surrounds us; it permeates everything in the universe." George Lucas studied the spirit and philosophy of Japanese martial arts and Asian philosophies when developing some of his themes. In centuries past, there was a melding of martial arts and religion, partly because many who practiced and studied martial arts were monks. Whether Buddhist or Shinto the monks were educated members of society. They were literate, religious and highly skilled in martial arts. Monks believed that a universal force existed; a power that they could summon, channel and with practice, call upon at will. They named that force Chi.

Chi is energy. Chi is light and dark. Chi is positive or negative. The first law of thermodynamics tells us that there is a finite amount of energy in the universe and that it is simply transformed from one type or form to another. The second law of thermodynamics tells us that systems require energy to maintain a state of equilibrium and that if they do not receive the input of essential energy they decay to a state of entropy. Thus, it takes energy to maintain your Chi in a positive state and a lack of positive energy allows Chi to decay or entropy easily into negative Chi or a negative state of being. Chi can transform from positive to negative. The balance of energy inside us can move from a positive state to a negative state or remain in a relative equilibrium, but the state of the Chi is never truly perfectly positive, negative, or neutral.

Negative energy is chaos and disorganization. It is lack of structure. Positive energy is structure. It is focused and directed. Chi manifests itself in chemical, electrical, thermal, kinetic and magnetic forms of energy. It is the "Dark side" as Lucas calls it and it is the "Light side". Chi is energy and it facilitates the flow of more of itself. The presence of positive energy facilitates the flow of more positive energy. Negative facilitates the flow of negative energy. When a person generates positive Chi it permeates those around him or her. The energy is transmitted from one to another just as the energy of the sun is transmitted to and absorbed by everything on Earth. When a person generates negative Chi it is transmitted to anything nearby and those nearby can absorb the negative energy.

The positive Chi is light, negative Chi is dark, they are the two intertwined halves of the yin yang. Negative energy is hard and forced; positive energy is soft and flows. They are the two opposing forces of the universe. The universe is equally balanced by the attraction of the opposites. As the cosmos spins out of control into the negative chaos caused by the big bang, it spawns positive organization of structured galaxies, solar systems and planets.

Positive Chi is peace and harmony. Negative Chi is war and discord. If you generate one or the other form of Chi you will receive it back. Energy and Chi continuously cycle throughout the universe. If we harbor negativity and negative thoughts, emotions and attitudes, they will attract more or their kind and these negative waves will continue and increase in magnitude indefinitely until positive is introduced and amplified enough to reverse the negative flow. The reason the Yin Yang has the tear-drop shape for the white and black side with the tail that shrinks to a point is to indicate that once you begin on the positive side or the other, then the wave of that type of energy can increase and magnify unless it begins to encounter some energy of the opposite type. Hence, the opposite-colored dot within each half of the Yin Yang.

Positive Chi, thoughts, and actions can multiply and will continue as long as you continue the cycle. There is a rhythm to the universe. Rhythm implies organization – a pattern that repeats itself. This pattern can be constructed of positive Chi or negative Chi. Either will cycle indefinitely until some energy of the opposite type begins to interrupt it. The positive can be turned into negative energy and the negative energy can be turned into positive energy. That is the symbolism behind the Chinese Yin Yang.

The Yin Yang is black and white, but each of the halves contains a small sphere of the opposite color. This is to represent the fact that the positive and negative energies can cycle independently and indefinitely. However, it is always possible that one form of energy or Chi can be corrupted or interrupted by some amount of the other. The Yin Yang reminds us that nothing exists in its pure state – at least not indefinitely. The promise of this is that a negative Chi can be interrupted and redirected by positive Chi and the positive Chi can begin to displace the negative Chi. It requires effort, skill, and energy to maintain either the positive or the negative. The ability to focus, channel, and direct positive or negative Chi requires effort to maintain in a perpetual cycle and there will be occasional interruptions, which will require effort to deflect. The positive and negative can balance each other and you may have a generally neutral Chi, but the point is that the polarity of your Chi shifts. It ebbs and flows according to your ability to maintain a balance and ideally to repel negative Chi.

The force that flows and binds the universe cannot be divided. The positive cannot be separated from the negative. One exists to define the other and one cannot exist without the other. A mountain peak only exists because there is a valley below it. The force is the combination of the positive and negative. The opposites will be drawn together and actions and attitudes that are negative will cause more negativity to be perpetuated and begin a negative cycle whose speed and magnitude will increase. Positive thoughts and actions will likewise increase in speed and magnitude. Your quest as a martial artist is to focus on generating and channeling positive Chi and deflecting negative Chi.

The teardrop of the white half of the Yin Yang begins small, at a single point to show us that we must begin small at a single point, with a single step. It shows us that we have much potential for good or bad and that we have the potential to work in either direction. The choice is ours.

Emotions

Have a passion about what you do when you train or spar, but do not involve emotions. A person can be emotional or rational, but not both at the same time.

A martial artist must use reason, intelligence, logic, experience, cunning, creativity, perception and many other qualities. However, these can all be easily blocked if you let emotions such as anger pervade your consciousness.

Being in an emotional state is a severe disadvantage to a martial artist, because it limits all of the other necessary qualities. It is a blocker of them. Emotion can be used to your advantage if you are able to evoke emotion such as anger or fear in your opponent. Then it will be easier to defeat because many of their critical martial qualities will be blocked and you have just reduced their fighting ability significantly.

Revenge

Revenge does not belong in the vocabulary of a martial artist. Revenge is a cancerous attitude for a martial artist to adopt, however warranted it may be.

Martial arts are not a training ground for vigilantes. The principles of martial arts and the integrity and character of a martial artist must reside on a higher moral plateau than a loathsome quality such as revenge. Martial arts are only for defense and the development of the mind, body and character of a person, not the degradation of the person. You must not use martial arts skill in a mercenary-like way to right a wrong. There are other avenues for this.

Attitude

Superior technique is of no use if you combine it with a bad attitude. A person with a good attitude and self-control but lesser technique can often defeat someone with a poor attitude and great technique. As I said earlier, attitude is a reflection of the internal spirit of the person.

- - - - - - - - - -

No attitude is worse than a bad attitude. A person must put some attitude of conviction behind their techniques if they expect their techniques to serve them.

Respect

Respect must be developed and maintained by the student. Respect aids self-discipline, which is essential to development and learning.

Respect is also the beginning of developing an open mind. Part of being open minded is respecting others ideas, people and styles without respect, very little is possible. However, it is easy to respect something or someone with which you agree. The challenge comes in trying to respect someone or something with which you do not agree. Respect other people and opinions without subjugating your own or allowing theirs to co-opt yours.

Etiquette

A martial artist is strong in character, personality and confidence. Fighting skill and strategy is assumed. Etiquette should be expected at any level.

Those who are high in skill, rank or experience should practice etiquette or courtesy and politeness with those who are less experienced and the converse as well.

Etiquette and courtesy is a sign of self-confidence, strength and security, not a sign of weakness or submissiveness. Respect is also an element of etiquette. Understand this well. All martial artists should practice this.

In the days of the Samurai and even in medieval Europe, warriors faced each other in mass or single combat, but they held a certain professional respect for each other; understanding that the skill of their opponents was acquired through much hard work, discipline, sacrifice and dedication. While two opponents or opposing forces might be enemies, their common ideals and traits as warriors engendered a mutual respect.

Ego

Guard your ego most carefully. It is a two-edged sword. Ego manifests itself as emotion. Emotions that are negative such as anger or hate will blind you when you are in the midst of battle or anywhere.

If ego becomes negative, emotions including fear, anger or hate will keep one from having an open mind. Without an open mind, the student of martial arts will wither and die from lack of new knowledge, thought and experiences.

A good fighter must be a good thinker and a good thinker only develops with an open mind to others and their ideas. Learn from and respect all others. Consider everything and you will grow in skill and knowledge.

Ego that manifests itself as positive emotion; self-confidence, pride, self-realization is a great thing. It is the key to building confidence and self-assuredness. A positive ego can give a fighter the conviction to overcome his or her own insecurity, doubt or fear of a superior opponent.

You must guard a positive ego as well as a negative ego. Do not be blatant or over-indulgent in a positive ego or you may disorient those around you. This is again, where balance is important. Develop balance and strength in these areas.

An Open Mind

Have an open mind to new styles, techniques and opinions of others. These things are not a threat. An open mind is strength and a security. A closed mind to new ideas will make them a greater threat because you will not benefit from what new people or ideas have to offer and they will be ahead of you in these areas.

An open mind is never bad because it develops awareness and awareness is essential to survival anywhere. When the mind is closed, it is unaware. When the mind is unaware, it is at risk.

Tradition and Innovation

Tradition and classical technique brought us to the present. Innovation and experimentation will take us into the future. Do not forget or lose tradition, or you will be fated to rediscover the reasons for it. Preserve tradition so that you will build upon it.

Tradition exists because at one time, to some extent, for some reason ... it worked! The purpose in studying and maintaining tradition is to see how what worked in the past may still have applicability in the present and how it can be improved upon for the future.

Make sure you are studying tradition to see how it worked and that you are not simply reenacting by rote without associating a meaning or purpose.

Know tradition, respect it, study it, and learn from it and from whence it came. We are here because of it, but do not be bound by it. To honor tradition as something sacred and immutable eliminates all hope for innovation. Without innovation, there is no possibility of improvement.

Martial Arts as Art Form

What are Karate, Kung Fu, Kendo or the other many styles? They are fighting systems; means of self-defense. However, we often forget in our training that they are most definitely art forms; the art of self-defense. An art form is a means of expression through some medium. For the painter, his medium may be oil paint on canvas or the sculptor may express him or herself through stone, clay, or porcelain. For the martial artist, his medium is himself, his physical movements and his character traits.

Artistic expression for other artists comes from the expression of their fears, hopes, joys and other emotions. Other artists have the freedom to express the full gamut of mental, physical or spiritual states. A martial artist seeks to develop his physical, mental and spiritual qualities to ever-higher levels so that he or she may express these highly developed characteristics.

Martial arts are indeed a unique art form. They are unlimited by the potential for development of the individual. It is in this endless, shapeless void of self-improvement, enlightenment and quest for inner-harmony that the martial artist finds his medium of expression. Consider this often.

Self-Reliance

A martial artist learns to depend upon no one. Self-reliance is necessary in self-defense, in training, in life. Do not always rely upon your instructor for everything. You must discover many things on your own. You must be the one with the self-discipline to continue even when you are tired or unmotivated.

Self-reliance applies to most areas of life. Depending upon others puts you in a more vulnerable position. Depending upon yourself gives you the best support you can find. If others come through, this is good, but do not rely upon them and you will never be disappointed.

Your self-reliance does not mean that you must cut yourself off or isolate yourself. You must simply handle all of the essentials yourself. After you have accounted for the essentials of your training, defense, or living, anything that others bring to you is an added bonus that you may appreciate because it is there, rather than miss because it is not.

Today, the mindset of many people is that someone else should be responsible; someone else should take care of me; someone else should be relied upon for the difficult things. This attitude is a weak, defeatist attitude. We must all learn to take responsibility for our actions, our well-being and our futures. This book is all about self-reliance. Rely on yourself, but engage the help of others as you pursue goals and dreams. You must expect more of yourself and less of others. This is the root of self-reliance.

Knowledge

You have knowledge when you know how to accomplish something, what came before us, or what you can do. Higher, true knowledge or meta-knowledge is when you know that you have certain knowledge. To know that you know something is the beginning of self-confidence and self-realization. Knowledge is a crucial resource that you will need to close the gaps between what you know now and what you need to know to accomplish your next goal or objective. Your mind should be continuously growing and challenged beyond your comfort zone. Knowledge is to the brain as air is to the lungs.

You need to determine what knowledge you need to acquire next; how to acquire it and what are your best modes of learning. Everyone learns differently; some by reading; some by watching; some by doing and some by a combination. Find what works and plan to always grow your knowledge some each day.

Knowledge can come from many sources, conversations, news media, books, magazines, the internet, experience, classroom instruction. Based on the types of knowledge you need, determine what sources area likely to provide that knowledge and begin to engage one or more of those sources each day.

Self-Confidence

Look at the word confidence. Its root is "confide". If you confide in someone else, you let him or her know something. If you confide in yourself, quietly, then you are letting yourself know.

If you have confided in yourself, then you have begun to develop self-confidence. You have begun to admit to yourself what it is that you really know. Until you can confide in yourself, you do not really have self-confidence.

Confidence is part of a positive ego. You cannot have a positive ego that is real without having confidence first. Confidence must be developed and kept sharp. Confidence is a skill that you must practice. Confidence begins with knowledge.

Integrity

Integrity is essential in the martial arts. It is the cornerstone of respect. Without integrity in an instructor, a student can have no respect for the instructor and will learn nothing.

At the core of integrity is honesty and trustworthiness. If a martial artist cannot be depended upon, then how can his or her teachings have meaning?

A person such as a doctor, who has the skill to save a life, must have integrity and be trustworthy. A person such as a martial artist, who has the skill to take a life must be trustworthy and of sound character.

Being a martial artist is a large responsibility that you cannot take lightly. For with the great skill and knowledge comes great responsibility. Consider this carefully.

Humility

You cannot develop respect truly without first developing humility. In many ways, humility is the first lesson in marital arts.

There is always someone better than you are. Accept this. Even if you are the best, someone else has useful knowledge that you do not have. If you were able to acquire this knowledge, then you would be even better than you are . . . even if you are already the best.

Humility is another skill that all martial artists must practice. It is the spirit of the martial arts. To have humility means that you have accepted your position and recognized that you are always in a position to improve or gain more knowledge or skill.

Until you have this humility, you cannot respect someone better or more knowledgeable than yourself. Without respecting them and opening your mind to what they have to offer, you will not be a true martial artist.

Conviction

This is the belief in what you are doing. It is not the same as self-confidence. When you have self-confidence, you know that you have the ability. When you have conviction, you believe that what you are doing is right.

In all aspects of using martial skill and strategy, you must have conviction about your actions. Conviction can be simple or complex. Simple conviction is believing that you are making the right move to counter your opponent because you have used this technique successfully in training.

Conviction can be more complex or on a higher plane in the sense that you may have a conviction that your actions in general (such as in a self-defense situation) are the right ones and you believe in the larger course of action or strategy that you have undertaken.

You must consider your convictions in many instances. With simple convictions, visualize yourself countering your opponent's advances. Decide in your mind beforehand whether or not your response to him would be appropriate or successful.

With complex convictions, consider where you stand on things that you have to deal with at some point. How far would you go in a self-defense situation or elsewhere?

Consider your convictions on many things often and early. If you wait until you find yourself in a situation, which requires action, you may have difficulty in choosing your path, because effective action usually comes from having strong convictions to accompany skill and strategy.

A martial artist must develop convictions as well as technique. Technique without conviction is a waste because conviction is the driving force required to make it work. Self-confidence; the knowledge that you can do something is not enough without conviction to push it through.

Determine your convictions. These will help you understand yourself better and know of what you are made.

Zanshin

Another Japanese martial concept is the idea of always being ready, always alert, always prepared for combat. In feudal Japan, prior to the battle of Seikegahara in 1877 which unified Japan under one leader, daily life for a Samurai meant that he could be attacked any time, anywhere. Samurai, developed specific techniques and positions for sitting so that they could quickly rise and draw their Katana or Wakazashi. This seated position required Samurai to fold their legs in such a way that from a seated position, they instantly had maximum muscle strength and leverage from both the upper and lower leg muscle groups and no wasted movement so that they cold rise for combat instantly.

Today this concept of Zanshin means that you must be mentally, physically and morally ready for combat or you must be ready to avoid combat either in the parking lot or on a battlefield. Remember, the greatest warriors are not war-like, but know when it is appropriate to summon their warrior spirit.

The Three Secrets to True Happiness

The story goes something like this . . .

A businessman was experiencing problems with his business, his personal life and marriage. He was not happy in many ways. Two of his close friends had told him of their experiences during a recent expedition to the mountains of the orient where they had found the three secrets of true happiness.

Disbelieving and skeptical, the businessman asked his friends the three secrets. They had returned energized, uplifted and enthusiastic and their businesses and personal lives had blossomed and flourished ever since they had returned.

They said that they could not tell him the secret, but they could tell him where he might discover it for himself. The businessman thought it over and decided to take their advice.

He took a leave of absence from work, said goodbye to his wife and children and left on a ship to the orient where his friends had gone. When he arrived, he contacted the mountain guides that his friends had recommended and prepared his hiking equipment.

They hiked for more than a week through the mountains until they reached the base of a mountain where the guides told him that near the summit was a Zen monastery. In this monastery was a great master who would be able to tell him the three secrets to true happiness.

He embarked on his own for the monastery. Upon arriving, he informed one of the priests why he was there. The priest told him that in three days he could meet with the Zen master. Until then he was to keep himself occupied and just wait.

He tried reading a book, but did not have the patience to read much. He walked around the beautiful gardens, but was bored, not even phased by the beauty and harmony that surrounded him. He was focused only on his anxiousness to meet with the master. He ate food with the other monks, but was annoyed that they ate in silence and would not speak with him as they focused on their food.

Finally, the day arrived when he could meet with the Zen master. All of the other monks were seated facing the master. One at a time, they would approach the master and bow reverently before asking a carefully selected question. After receiving their answer, they would return to where they had been seated and reflect on the answer they had been given.

When the businessman's turn came, he approached the master. He said that he had traveled across the ocean, hiked through the mountains and spent three days in anxious anticipation of finding out the three secrets of true happiness. The master responded that he would tell the businessman the three secrets.

The master said, "The first secret to true happiness is to pay attention. The second secret of true happiness is to pay attention. The third secret to true happiness is to pay attention."

The businessman looked at the master in disbelief. "You mean that I came all the way here for you to tell me to pay attention ... that's it? Those are the three secrets to true happiness?" He inquired.

The master said, "Give these time and consider them well." He then dismissed the businessman.

Furious, the businessman returned to his home country, to his family and business. He was angry with his friends for having made him go all the way for such nonsense. Weeks went by and the businessman got back into his usual routine and assumed his daily activities as he had before. Nothing was any different.

Then one day while caught in traffic, he began to think about his adventure to the orient. He began to consider what the Zen master had said. How could the master have been so serious about such a simple answer? It struck him suddenly. There were so many things in his daily life that he simply overlooked or ignored.

The very things of life were all around him, nature, beauty and happiness, but he was blind to it because he could not focus and pay attention long enough. He began to pay attention to everything, to the color of an autumn leaf, the veins in the leaf, its shape and size and how it differed from others.

He paid complete attention to every detail that he could experience in everything. He noticed the simple beauty in nature around him and in his children and wife and their daily events and accomplishments. He noticed things that he had never seen, by simply paying attention to the smallest things, the tiniest details. He gave his undivided attention to everything and everyone in his life.

By giving his attention, he could see, solve, and understand problems, relationships and situations so much more easily than before. His business began to improve, his marriage became more fulfilling, he enjoyed his friends more and life in general had begun to change completely, simply by paying attention and doing just one thing at a time.

As you learn to focus and reflect, you will be able to consider more clearly things that you encounter. In your daily activities, you will be more focused on them and hopefully more successful at them. This is what the monks call, eating when you eat, working when you work, sleeping when you sleep.

Appreciation

The Koreans call it "Kamsah". When I was a White Belt, I learned the White Belt pattern under the Jhoon Rhee system of American Tae Kwon Do. He named the pattern "Kamsah Hyung". After graduating to Gold Belt, Grandmaster Rhee came to the graduation ceremony to watch the students and speak about martial arts. He explained the simplicity and the significance of "Kamsah Hyung". He explained that appreciation was something that a student must learn to have for himself and to show toward his or her instructor for taking the time and care to share his knowledge with the student.

Learn to appreciate where you are and what you have accomplished. If you stop for a moment to reflect on your level of skill and progress you will have a good sense of where you are and where you should go. If you cannot appreciate what you have gained, then you have gained nothing.

The Quest for Purpose: The Servant-Warrior

I have discussed that every move must have a purpose in the sense of strategy, but purpose has a higher meaning. You must discover your purpose.

Ultimately, discovering purpose begins with finding your passion. When you have found the things about which you are truly passionate and the things that you are good at doing, you have begun to discover your purpose. The things that you are passionate about will be fulfilling and to be fulfilled and achieve a sense of purpose you must be involved in something greater than yourself.

The term Samurai means one who serves. A warrior is a servant. In feudal Japan, the Samurai served society as warriors in time of war and as government officials and community leaders at all levels. The concept of servant-warrior existed in medieval Europe with the knights of various countries. These knights were warriors, and they served something bigger than themselves. Many protected and defended the weak, the poor and the sick. The Knights Hospitallers founded the first hospitals to care for the sick and injured in the Holy Land.

Today a warrior spirit is just as critical and the servant quality of the warrior ethos must be developed and practiced in daily life. The warrior must be willing to fight for whatever is right. In today's modern world, there is just as much need as in ancient times for a true warrior. A warrior is someone who may have the skill and conviction to take a life in a thousand different ways if necessary, but who is willing to protect, defend and improve the lives of those in need.

A police officer is a warrior who is trained to kill if necessary, but is sworn to serve and protect. A soldier is trained to fight and kill, but is prepared to provide humanitarian assistance after a disaster or to help rebuild a war-torn region. A firefighter has the tenacity and skill to combat a raging inferno, but is moved to comfort those experiencing tragedy and loss.

Finding purpose or your life's mission helps remove dissonance, and reduce stress while providing clarity and direction. Dissonance keeps all aspects of your life from being in balance and harmony with one another. When you have discovered your purpose and a good many important aspects of your life are in harmony, you are becoming fulfilled and complete. This is not mystical or religious. It is simply balancing the elements of your life and paying complete attention to each of them in turn. It is maintaining you, yourself, who you are and what you are with focus, persistence and consistency. To omit this balance or to cease to maintain this balance is to allow who or what you are to begin to decay and to allow your Chi to flow toward the negative. This decay may have many manifestations. It may be physical, spiritual, moral, political, intellectual or otherwise.

As I have already said, balance is important in many aspects. As you define and discover your purpose, you will also discover the aspects of your life, which enable you to fulfill your purpose in different ways. It is a never-ending quest.

Your purpose or goals can change over time as you redefine it or as you begin to see it more clearly. Whatever its form, it should involve some element of service to some aspect of society. Even a non-martial artist can become a warrior of sorts in the pursuit of his mission. Many famous figures throughout history have pursued a cause that at its center helped others in some way. Clara Barton, founder of the American Red Cross, felt compelled by her faith to be a servant to those injured on the battlefield and later to anyone displaced or impacted by disasters and in need of compassion and emergency relief. William Booth a London minister founded the Salvation Army. Goodwill was founded by a Methodist minister who believed in giving people a hand up, not a hand out. United Way was founded by a priest, two ministers and a rabbi and was intended to act as a funding agent to support various charities and has coordinated relief efforts for millions of people since its inception. Habitat for Humanity was founded by Christian missionaries simply to solve the problem of decent housing for the poor and has built more than 300,000 homes in 3000 communities across the world. Chuck Norris created the Kickstart Foundation to help children succeed in school and in life through martial arts training, discipline and traditional values.

Major William (Bill) Hendricks (USMC Reserve) started Toys for Tots. That first Christmas the Major and some other Marine Reservists in Los Angeles delivered 5000 toys to need children on Christmas Eve. Since then the Marine Corps has adopted the program and has expanded the original goal of bringing the joy of

Christmas to America's needy children to include humanitarian objectives of rebuilding self-esteem and mentoring children living in poverty by exposing them to the positive examples set by the U.S. Marines who distribute toys to them each Christmas. From 1947 through 2000, Marines distributed in excess of 272 million toys to more than 133 million needy children throughout the United States. The spirit of Santa is alive and well!

John Walsh, host of the long-running television show "America's Most Wanted" suffered the horrific loss of his six-year-old son who was murdered. John was motivated to start the television series and help other parents and victims of violent crimes find justice. John's loss was turned into a positive gain for society. His singular efforts have changed the way police departments across the country pursue and track violent criminals. In his case, John's passion found him. Your passion may be planned or it may be purely accidental. It really doesn't matter as long as you are truly passionate about what you are doing it will never seem like work.

There are countless examples of these brave souls who had a vision and pursued it with unwavering tenacity and determination and made a difference. Their mission may have involved direct service to individuals or indirectly through the creation of services, inventions, medicines, technologies or social changes that improved the quality and safety of life. In every case, these intrepid individuals were warriors in every way.

You may study some of history's success stories for ideas, or try volunteer service in a variety of areas simply for the experience. Be a benefit to others. Serve your community, your church or your neighborhood schools or youth groups. Find a charity to support. Teach an illiterate adult to read, become involved in your local government, hospital or some type of mission work locally or elsewhere. In the process of these experiences, you may discover what you have been seeking. It is not all about you. It IS about you and your relationship to others.

Finding a purpose you can serve will make you a better warrior. Apply that passion and drive and you will be positioning yourself for real success; the stuff of legend. No one ever cared about the greedy narcissist who kept his wealth stashed away and focused only on himself and his material possessions and creature comforts. Self-focus is a formula for self-destruction, but history does record and celebrate the annals of those who apply their energies to making a positive impact on the lives of others. Don't get me wrong, there is nothing inherently wrong with having an expensive home, exotic cars, large sums of financial assets and all the creature comforts that one might desire. What I am saying is that if that is your sole pursuit; your end game; the pinnacle of your aspirations; then you will ultimately never be truly happy. You will never achieve a full realization of your potential humanity. You will be a consumer only, but not a producer of anything of worth. That worth is not measured in terms of what you hold dear and valuable, but what you can contribute of your own industry that is of real and lasting worth to others.

There is an important caveat; however, your service and the choice to do something that is of value to yourself as well as others must be voluntary, not required. Volunteering to serve in some capacity provides an opportunity for you to mature. There is no maturity or expression of humanity in being required by law or force to serve – that is conscription and totalitarianism. Those are the mandates thrust upon people by the likes of Chairman Mao. Forced or required service is not the action or will of a free people. Greater virtue lies in service that is given willingly than in service that is taken forcefully. Giving freely is honorable. A free people should not be forced or required to follow a certain course of action even if it is for the best of causes, too much blood has been spilled fighting to preserve the freedom to make our own choices.

All during this process of finding your purpose, you will be trying to maintain some semblance of balance between the different aspects of yourself and your life. There will be times when you maintain a better balance than at others. The important thing is to recognize when you have an imbalance and adjust it.

Another Zen story helps illustrate this. . . A student asked a Zen master, what is Zen? The master answered, "Zen is eating when you eat, working when you work, and resting when you rest." The student was surprised. Master, that is too simple. Yes, said the master. However, almost no one is able to do this.

You must prioritize your activities and pay attention to each of them in turn so that each task, act, and situation is worthy of your complete attention so that it will be accomplished to its fullest, before moving on to the next.

You must realize that you may also never really feel that you have discovered your purpose, but seeking out the opportunities for service and kindness and generosity in large ways and in small ways is the soft half of the warrior. It is the Yin, to the warrior-fighter of the Yang. Move in the direction of what you sense or perceive to be your purpose. Even if it is not, at least you know now, not to pursue that course again.

You may try a direction or a path that you sense is right and it may turn out otherwise. That is ok. Every time you must retrace your steps from a wrong path, you have helped in some small way to better define your purpose. Even if it is by defining what is NOT your purpose or goal.

Zen

There has been a tremendous amount of talk about Zen. Books have been written about Zen. Monks devote themselves and many martial artists and their styles place a high value on Zen, but what is it? Why is it so important? Is it important?

I have concluded that Zen has many manifestations including many religious connotations, but at its core is a simple pursuit; the pursuit of internal harmony within yourself and external harmony between yourself, others and nature. Zen has an infinite number of manifestations. Until you have a good degree of internal harmony, you cannot have external harmony. Until you have external harmony, you cannot have harmony with nature or even begin to contemplate your place in it.

The internal harmony begins with this enlightenment. From this state of internal harmony, you can begin to develop a greater harmony with your surroundings and those with whom you interact. There is no secret formula to achieve Zen. Many people achieve a state of Zen without even knowing it. It has to do with developing a clear sense of who you are and how you fit in. Zen is about reaching a point of self-enlightenment and discovering your purpose. How you can best achieve your purpose. I say self-enlightenment because Zen cannot be taught or explained . . . it must be discovered and experienced. A Zen master can only guide the student toward self-enlightenment, not enlighten the student directly. As with many things, the student must climb the mountain himself.

There are many stories and techniques for guiding a student in the direction where they can discover their own Zen ... that is the role of the Zen master. He knows the way to Zen, but he cannot give it to you as a college professor can give you the laws of Physics. Zen is more personal than that. That is the perennial mystery and misunderstanding of many who seek Zen. Zen works because you make your own discoveries and find out what you need to know for yourself. This knowledge or enlightenment applies to you alone. The enlightenment that you experience cannot be shared or passed on to another because they must develop their own understanding and harmony, not merely take on yours. That is the key.

Enlightenment

When you have discovered the secret to a new technique, ask yourself if you have become enlightened. Have you, or have you simply discovered a long known secret already known to others? When are you enlightened? When do you feel it?

Enlightenment may be permanent or momentary. It is permanent when you realize that you are not merely acquiring knowledge about something outside or apart from you, but when you realize that you have just developed a new perspective or understanding of something inside yourself.

Learning outside things, math, science, and self-defense is not enlightenment. It is simply acquiring knowledge. It is good and useful, but it is not enlightenment. Knowledge is the illumination of the outside world; enlightenment is the illumination of the inner world of the self.

The soul of the martial artist begins dark; void of self-understanding. As the discovery and understanding of the self begins, the soul and character of the martial artist is formed and illuminated from within.

- - - - - - - - - -

Can you keep the soul always concentrated from straying?
Can you regulate the breath and become soft and pliant like an infant?
Can you clear and get rid of the unforeseen and be free from fault?
Can you become enlightened and penetrate everywhere without knowledge?

- - - - - - - - - -

The best soldier is not soldierly. The best fighter is not ferocious;
The best conqueror does not take part in war;

- - - - - - - - - -

The weakest things in the world can overmatch the strongest things in the world.

Noting in the world can be compared to water for its weak and yielding nature; yet in attacking the hard and the strong nothing proves better than it, for there is no alternative to it.

The weak can overcome the strong and the yielding can overcome the hard; this all the world knows but does not practice.

- - - - - - - - -

He who knows others is wise,
He who knows himself is enlightened.
He who conquers others is strong,
He who conquers himself is mighty.
He who knows contentment is rich.
He who keeps on his course with energy has will,
He who does not deviate from his proper place will long endure.
He who may die but not perish has longevity.

from - Tao Te Ching

by   - Lao Tzu

Honor

Honor is very much the sum total and the result of the cultivation and development of all of the other qualities of a martial artist that I have described. You achieve honor when you are respected as a servant-warrior. This can only happen through successful and sincere development of your warrior spirit. The respect you earn is not a right that you are guaranteed, but a privilege that you must maintain.

Simply acquiring rank and experience does not make the martial artist worthy of honor. There are many high-ranking fighters of dubious or questionable character. You can become worthy of honor when you personify the qualities that I have described in this book.

Honor belongs to the individuals who uphold these qualities with sincerity and consistency. An honorable person is not honorable only when inside the dojo, but is also honorable outside, where there are many influences that may challenge that person's integrity. Honor means causing no harm to others; except in a self-defense situation where there is no means of escape or avoidance. Some cultures talk of honor killings in order to prevent embarrassment or committing seppuku because of some apparent disgrace. This is not honor, this is frustration with some shortcoming or undesired outcome. Nonetheless, to kill oneself or another in the name of honor is only a disgrace and an admission of failure. True honor is found in learning from the situation and improving in the future. Growing in character is honorable.

Chapter **5**

Success for Life

Finding and Following Your Passion

"To achieve your dreams you must leave your comfort zone and never return."
        Kevin Brett

Success: Some Assembly Required

An overnight success is generally years in the making

One of the other co-founders and President of United Karate used to say, "The only martial arts secret I've discovered is a four letter word called *work*." You cannot achieve success or excellence in anything without effort. There are no shortcuts. That doesn't mean you have to work yourself to the point of exhaustion or stress over it, but effort is certainly required; as is sacrifice.

If you have ever purchased a new computer desk or do-it-yourself entertainment center, or some other item that comes to you in a box with many pieces, just remember that famous line on the box that says, "Some assembly required." Think of your goals and dreams in the same way, "Some assembly required." Oh, and don't forget the other famous line, "Batteries not included." You must supply the energy and positive Chi to get there.

So what is success? Like all of the other terms that I have defined and analyzed in this book, success is just another word that everyone throws around. In my own personal journey, I have enjoyed a number of instances of what I view as success. I have been a jazz saxophone player since age seven. Throughout my school years, I practiced diligently and was selected as a member of an elite all-county jazz band in high school. I applied a positive attitude, enthusiasm and commitment to practice and improve my abilities. The fact that I was chosen for that group was a success. I had a passion, I followed it and it paid off.

Later, after graduation, I formed a jazz big band with nineteen musicians and a singer. We played numerous shows around the metropolitan area and the band continued for several years even after I left. That was a success; following a passion and realizing the objective of running that organization as we did. We set out to accomplish a tangible outcome and did.

I just recently finished a four-year stint as a Scout leader where I ran a Scouting organization that at one point had more than one hundred Scouts and twenty-four Scout leaders. For four years running, we were the most highly decorated unit of our type in the local district. We held many very involved events, which really helped the boys grow and learn valuable skills and character traits. They had excellent experiences and we had very high participation in all of the events during my tenure. The outdoors and Scouting are two passions of mine and I shared that with my son and daughters and many others who benefited from my passion. This was another success.

My problem is that I have too many passions, so I have to limit myself and try to focus on one or two at a time. There is a season for everything. We don't have to become schizophrenic and try to do everything at the same time. Apply the discipline to remain focused and you will see results and achieve happiness.

Here's an example of what I'm talking about. Today parents feel that good parenting means signing up each child for several sports and activities in and out of school simultaneously. The reality is that somewhere in the mix, homework looses priority and children and parents become stressed. I have seen too many instances where a parent has to whisk their child away from a soccer game before it is over to take them to a baseball game. Other times, on many occasions, I have seen a parent take a child to a two-night campout beginning on a Friday night. The next morning they leave before breakfast to go to a basketball game. They return to camp around lunchtime to participate for an hour or two in the camp activities only to leave again in the mid-afternoon to go to a football game. Then they return after dinner to hang around the campfire, listening like some outsider to the other campers talk about the fun events of the day. What is my point? Well, if it is not already clear, the child does not complete any event or activity. Where is the sense of pride in accomplishment in that? The child cannot really feel like he or she is part of any of the groups because there are too many conflicting and overlapping activities. The child develops little of their potential because they simply do not have the time to become good at anything and actually enjoy it. Their parents are merely helping the child check a box.

The smart approach would be to limit the activities to one sport and one other activity per season. Over time, the child will still be able to participate in a variety of activities or sports, just not all at once! It seems obvious, but I have friends who have been doing this insane multi-taking for years and keep talking about how difficult and stressful it is. I have seen children at very young ages talk about how overwhelmed they are; sounding like some over-worked government employee who is trying to do the work of three people. I tell the parents to just stop, but they don't seem to feel that they have it within their power to run their lives instead of letting their lives run them. A little focus with some prioritization will make life more balanced and enjoyable. Children and adults need this so that they can focus on fewer goals that they may actually achieve and gain that sense of confidence and accomplishment they seek. That is a path toward greater happiness.

In my office, I have a picture frame on the wall that is a reminder to me about the value and importance of focus, perseverance and determination. The certificate in that frame, like my first-degree black belt, took much longer to earn than I would have hoped, but the experience was an object lesson in determination. Like the quest to complete my first-degree black belt, the experience changed my life. The frame contains my Bachelor's degree.

Many people have Bachelor's degrees and not many of them are worth much unfortunately, because people do not always use them to reach their potential. They are often merely a ticket to a job, not a stepping-stone in a personal journey. To me, my degree is different. I earned it twenty-four years after I began it. There were many points along the way where I had to stop for various reasons; some by choice and some not. The dream and the desire never left me nor did the determination. The result was that I completed that academic marathon and it has made a huge difference in my life and career. It has brought opportunities and helped me develop more character along the way. It was not always easy, but nothing really worth doing ever is. This is success; but you must recognize your successes so that you can build upon them. The attainment of my degree was not the real measure of success. The success was the change in me and the character and perseverance that I developed to complete that quest.

Throughout my professional career, I have maintained my usual optimistic attitude and mindset of success to carry me through difficult technical and management challenges in the information technology field. I have been handed numerous projects that were failing or at high risk. Other people had thrown in the towel on these projects or could not envision a successful outcome. I did my homework, learned and honed the skills that I needed and applied them with a "failure is not an option" mentality.

Typically I applied optimism, sheer force of will and a clearly articulated vision of what we were going to accomplish and how. With this approach, I was able to lead and motivate teams of software engineers, designers, and developers to meet or exceed our objectives. Those various efforts were successes. The combination of skill, experience, vision and mindset carried the team and me through the challenges to realize our goals. We also had a lot of fun in the process!

Later in my career, I evolved from a software engineer role into an enterprise architect role and IT director. Without getting into the technicalities, enterprise architecture is concerned with understanding and modeling all of the business activities, information, systems and infrastructure of an organization and evaluating how well the organization's activities and investments align to the enterprise's goals.

I have built and managed enterprise architectures for corporate and federal clients. These efforts represent the structure of entire federal agencies, all of their inner workings and external interactions. The complexity is immense and the challenges to understand and help transform a complex enterprise are significant. In each instance I communicated a clear vision of what was possible, injected what many described as an infectious optimism and lead teams to overcome some very difficult challenges. I applied my black belt determination to get the job done. Ultimately, these efforts resulted in a series of successes that inspired the teams and the clients to tackle the largest organizational and operational problems facing them.

So why am I describing all of these things, because these events and outcomes and journeys are all examples of success. They do not involve material wealth, but they are characterized by successful outcomes and realization of a vision. The completion and publication of this book is a success. The main chapters of this book were actually written in 1996 before we first opened United Karate. Originally, this book was called *The Book of Strategy*. Later when I decided to expand it and add to the original content, I realized that it was far more than simply a text on strategy. Now, twelve years after the original spiral-bound version was available for sale at our school, you are reading this published version. Have you noticed that I have a tendency to take my time accomplishing things? I guess I don't like to feel rushed, he said sarcastically!

The point in sharing these experiences is to show you some real life examples of success; to help re-calibrate your thinking and your perception of success. Sure it's great to have lots of money and material things, but just don't confuse those possessions with success; they are not. Success is a way of life that starts with a mindset and a way of approaching goals and challenges. It is not about achieving financial wealth and material possessions. Those things are detractors and cloud the real success and accomplishments. Possessions and financial wealth are occasional by-products of some types of success; they are not success itself.

There are many other examples that I could provide about successes I have experienced and enjoyed, but the point is that I adopted a success-oriented mindset that I could apply to any goal, vision or dream. These goals can be small or large; it does not matter. Apply the principles to everything you do. When you are able to do this, you will start to experience the real successes that make life worth living.

There seems to be a cultural cliché that is tacitly understood by all of us as to what we mean when we say someone is successful. Let's look at a few of the popular examples of what many people think success is and then we'll look at some examples of what success can be.

We often think of success as someone who is wealthy, popular, attractive, talented, artistic, or athletic. Those people who have many enviable possessions like expensive cars, huge homes, high-paying jobs and all the other common trappings that we often think of as the hallmarks of success.

For the most part, if you have a well-paying job it is because you have a significant amount of education in some very marketable skills or at least you know someone well connected who was able to help you get that job. If you are athletic and have won sports competitions, especially in individual sports such as swimming, martial arts, running, tennis, and others then you have trained long and hard to develop those skills. If you are artistic, you may have been born with some degree of vision, but you still had to invest the time to learn the mechanics of how to produce high quality art that is capable of expressing whatever it is you want to express.

The point is that when we see successful people, we only see the tip of the iceberg. What we are not seeing is the years of work, training, practice, ups and down, smaller successes and setbacks that those people experienced and overcame to get where they are today. It is the hidden part of success that you need to grasp and embrace that will help you achieve the visible part of success.

Ralph Waldo Emerson gave us a down to earth and non-materialistic perspective on success…

> To laugh often and much;
> To win the respect of intelligent people
> And the affection of children,
> To earn the appreciation of honest critics
> And endure the betrayal of false friends;
> To appreciate beauty, to find the best in others,
> To leave the world a bit better
> Whether by a healthy child a garden patch,
> Or a redeemed social condition;
> To know that even one life has breathed easier
> Because you lived.
> This is to have succeeded.

There is an elegant simplicity and humility to the success of which Emerson speaks. You almost sense the peaceful, tranquility of his vision when you read the passage above. Does Emerson's vision of success mean that we all need to move to a foreign land, open an orphanage, and live the life of Mother Theresa; no, noble and charitable as that would be. Certainly, she was immensely successful in doing just that and saved many children from the brink of starvation and other terrible fates.

Whatever your definition of success, there is a vision behind it. There is some idea, goal or state of accomplishment that you view as success. Earning your black belt is certainly a success in martial arts, but the greater success is to embrace and embody the positive concepts and character traits of a martial artist and a servant-warrior that I discussed in the earlier chapters.

When you earn a black belt, you have acquired a great power. The power to kill, injure, maim or not kill; and with great power comes great responsibility. I hope that simply *earning* a black belt is not the sum total of your martial arts goals, but that *being* a black belt is what you aspire to. There is a world of difference.

What I am talking about when we discuss success is what you plan to make of the future. What will today hold? How will it bring you closer to your goals and what will you do to become excellent?

One of my favorite quotes about moving forward and driving toward the future comes from Walt Disney when he was being interviewed about the Florida project, which was later renamed Walt Disney World. He said, "Why talk about the future if you're not going to build it?" That is an attitude of success.

It's All in Your Head

Dreams are the blueprints of success

Henry Ford said, "If you think you can't, you're right. If you think you can, you're right." What is it about some people that make them seem to exude success? Why do some people seem to have the Midas touch where everything turns to gold? Successful people have developed certain traits and qualities that enable them to have a dream, chase it and realize that dream. They still have setbacks, off-days, moments of frustration and despair, but they keep at it. They persevere.

If you have earned your black belt, then you know what perseverance is about. If you are a marathon runner, you know about drive and determination. Whatever the accomplishment, you will always notice that successful people are positive and optimistic. You cannot achieve success with negativity and pessimism. That is the antithesis of success. Nothing great was ever accomplished with pessimism. Start programming yourself to achieve goals rather than overcome by obstacles and setbacks.

Look around at people you know or people whom you have encountered throughout your life. Now, think about the ones whom you would say are not successful and then think about the ones whom you would say are successful. Notice that in almost every instance the successful ones are upbeat, driven, positive, encouraging and supportive of others who are trying to achieve goals and dreams. That is because they understand that it takes a positive mindset and they're having fun enjoying their success. Keeping the positive Chi going and flowing requires effort and constant positive inputs of more positive Chi.

Those people who are not particularly successful are also generally not very happy or positive. Their attitude is holding them back. They are not negative or pessimistic because they are unsuccessful. They are unsuccessful because they are negative and pessimistic. Get your cause and effect straight! Success does not make you happy. Happiness and a positive attitude enable you to become successful.

One of the most important traits of successful people is visualization. I discussed this earlier. It is important to be able to visualize your response to some opponent. As you train you must visualize how you will perform a kata or some other activity. Visualizing a dream is the first step toward achieving it.

You cannot just *have* a dream; you must *see* it. It must seem completely real to you. Many interviews and studies by psychologists and business school programs have found that successful people differ from the rest in at least one key respect. Successful people claim to visualize their dreams very realistically, in full color and in three-dimensions. They are able to see their accomplishment as if it is right in front of them. To these people the dream is already a reality in their mind's eye and their next step is to carry out the actions to make the reality in their life match the reality inside their mind. For these people, success is a state of mind more than it is a matter of individual circumstances. They carry their dream in their head everywhere they go and constantly revisit it and savor it. They want it bad and you must want it bad too!

There are countless examples of people who have become astronauts, Presidents, real-estate tycoons, Olympic athletes, entertainers, scholars and exemplary people of all professions and pursuits. These people did not begin wealthy, they did not start out as Olympic athletes, and they did not begin life with a large real-estate portfolio or a Nobel Prize. They changed their daily routines and focused their efforts on the prize, the end game. They pursued excellence at every turn. I know, it's trite, but you cannot win the game if you don't play.

My son loves to play his video games. He spends more time than I would like for him to, playing these games, but what I have noticed is that he stays focused on the objectives of the game. The more he practices, the better he becomes. As he improves his skill in a particular game, he accomplishes goals at the initial level, which enable him to move to the next level. As he continues to maintain his focus, he works his way up the levels until he has successfully completed the highest level and wins the game – achieving his goal. I try to use this example to encourage him to apply the same strategies with his schoolwork and every other part of his life. To achieve success you must stay focused, and work every day toward your goals to move on to the next level.

Pushing the Envelope
"Do not try. ... Do."
    Yoda

Unless you are a homeless person, you can likely say you have achieved some degree of success in your life. If you are comfortable to some extent with your level of income or the home you live in or the car you drive, then you have achieved some measure of success; and this is your worst enemy. You run the risk of being too comfortable. Because of your current level of comfort, you may not be driven to excel beyond your current situation.

If you have achieved first-degree black belt and you are comfortable with this, then further success in martial arts may be hindered because you may not be inclined to continue advancing your studies or teaching others. This is where many students think they have reached the top of the mountain and stop climbing.

Too many things can get in the way of your dreams. Go around them. Keep focused on your goals. Do not be stalled out by little things. Remember every goal can be broken down into very small pieces that can be approached and conquered one at a time. If you break anything down far enough, then you can accomplish the smaller pieces and enjoy a string of on-going successes.

There will always be negative people. Surround yourself with those who are supportive and are willing to help you rather than drag you down. Read inspiring books and copy down positive and encouraging quotes and review them often to keep driving you forward. Do not allow people around you to ridicule your goals or dreams. They are *your* dreams, not theirs. They have no business raining on your parade. You must allow only optimism to guide you and an unwavering belief in your ability to accomplish your dream.

You may not have the ability to carry out your goals when you begin. If you did, then whatever you are seeking would not be a goal. Achieving goals is about closing gaps; gaps in skill, knowledge, excellence and resources. Just because you lack a certain skill, knowledge, financial or physical resource does not mean that you cannot acquire it. You must plan a way to borrow, rent, share, trade or buy what you need.

As I discussed in the passage on Chi in the previous chapter, being negative is easy. The positive Chi takes effort to maintain and reversing the natural tendency to be negative requires effort. All this effort requires us to leave our comfort zone. That is really the key to success. To achieve your dreams you must leave your comfort zone and never return. That may seem scary at first and it may not be completely appealing. The question is, are you content where you are? You have a goal, dream, or vision. You obviously have this goal because it is something you wish to accomplish. Do you really want to abandon your dream and spend the rest of your life in the purgatory of regret? I don't think so.

> *"People who have given up are ruled by their darkest mistakes, worst failures, and deepest regrets. If you want to be successful, then be governed by your finest thoughts, your highest enthusiasm, your greatest optimism, and your most triumphant experiences."*
> *John C. Maxwell*

Each day you have the opportunity to do something. That something can take you closer or further from your goals. The choice is yours. There will be days when you do not feel the optimism or seem to lack the energy or drive. That's ok. You are not Superman. You are not a machine and you will never be perfect, but you can be better and better until you become excellent. Success is a gradual process. Expect much of yourself, but also realize that there will be off-days or valleys. Find your inspiration at those times and don't allow yourself to get stuck in those valleys. Look back on how far you have come and use that positive momentum to push you up out of the valley and onward.

If you let small things get in your way, you will easily loose sight of your goals. The thing that is different about a martial artist is how he or she puts setbacks in perspective. To put them in the proper perspective, you must first recognize them for what they are. A setback is just that. It is not a defeat or failure unless you make it one. It is temporary, not permanent. If your state of mind is such that a setback is a permanent obstruction between you and your purpose or goals, then it will be permanent. Remember Henry Ford's words. "If you think you can't, you're right." That is one time you don't want to be right.

I had been training for four years and was an advanced brown belt. I had learned the curriculum, practiced, and trained diligently. I was nearing the point when I would be ready to test for my novice black belt; the rank before first-degree black belt. One day at my apartment, I severed a nerve and two tendons in the palm of my right hand on a piece of broken pottery. The injury required the efforts of a hand surgeon who stitched the nerve back together and repaired the tendons. I spent the next year going through intensive physical therapy just to regain the use of my hand. It was painful and certainly not fun.

During that time, I could not practice martial arts. I simply had to wait. I had to become healthy again and allow the injury heal completely. During the year that I was out, the school changed their curriculum and I was told that I would not be able to finish what I had started and test under the old curriculum. I could keep my advanced brown-belt rank, but would have to learn the entire new curriculum from white belt.

Here I thought I was so close to being ready for novice black belt only to find that I had to start all over again. I accepted that setback, but told myself that I wanted my black belt. That was the goal I had set and I was not going to let that change of curriculum deter me. I began learning the new curriculum. After a year of no training or physical activity, I had to begin my conditioning again.

I used the four years of martial arts training that I had to that point to help me learn the new curriculum and become better than I had been at the old curriculum. The additional time allowed me to improve my technique and other skills. I was not really starting from scratch. I dived in, worked through the curriculum until I was ready for my novice black belt test. I passed that test with high marks and went on eighteen months later to pass my first-degree black belt test.

I had been an advanced brown belt for four years; a rather long time. The way I saw it, I was marinating. I wanted to be well-seasoned when I finally did become a black belt. All together, it took eight long years to earn my first-degree black belt. It seemed like forever. The wait was well worth it.

You must deal with setbacks and remove them or work through them to succeed. In my case, I was not about to let anything short of permanent and complete physical incapacity prevent me from earning my black belt. The belt was not important to me. It was the fact that I had set a goal and it was the principle of completing it. I was not going to let myself down. To give up would have been failure and that was not part of my plan. Success was my objective. It is not so much what the problem is, but how you deal with it.

Some people seem to have a shorter distance to go than others do when it comes to reaching their goals. Some people set out to do what they have decided and accomplish their goal with relative ease. Circumstances for them may be more favorable at times. If your circumstances are not very favorable, you can take steps to change them and get on the path toward your goals.

Other people attempting the same goal may take much longer and suffer many setbacks as I did, but it is the process of addressing the setbacks and taking them on that is the real accomplishment. Achieving the goal is simply a milestone that signifies that you have overcome all of the setbacks and obstacles you have encountered.

It is never too late to achieve your dreams, but do not delay. Do not waste time. Age is not generally an issue. Unless you have a dream to become an Olympic Gold Medalist in the one-hundred meter dash and you are in your seventies, it's probably a good bet that your goal is a little unrealistic. However, that doesn't mean that you cannot adjust your goal somewhat and still take up running if that is your passion. You just have to tweak your goal a little and adopt a different, but related goal such as distance running or maybe speed walking or hiking. That is why you need to take time to write down your goal, think about it and make sure that you have really written down the right goal. Once you have refined your thinking and are certain of your destination, then you can begin and know where you are headed and why.

I have taught students who were age five and literally had a gentleman who began his martial arts studies at age fifty-five; earning his black belt seven years later. Many awesome goals are achieved later in life. Recently a seventy-one year old man climbed Mount Everest. I don't recall if he actually made it all the way to the summit, but I hope that at that age I can muster the determination and tenacity that he did to go as far as he did.

The Real Deal

As I said, there are goals or dreams that are likely to never be realized and which require some modification or realignment, but success is still possible. At United Karate, we had two very special students who each had the heart of a lion. One young woman had cerebral palsy with greatly reduced use of her hands and feet. The other woman had muscular dystrophy and was wheelchair-bound. They did not exactly fit the profile of your typical martial arts students bound for black belt.

They were friends and decided that they simply wanted to sign up and get what they could out of the program. We the instructors worked with both of them and devised an approach to training them. These women were simply determined to learn strategies to defend themselves and to find a form of exercise that would challenge them and possibly improve their physical condition.

Both of them trained diligently and gained increased strength, stamina and dexterity. We were all amazed at their progress.

It was awesome to see the student with CP gain mobility and coordination. No one predicted that as an outcome. To her, that was a huge success. She realized that she would never be able to execute the various techniques required for the black belt test, but she had made dramatic progress from her original disposition. He goal was not the belt, it was the character and determination that must be developed to earn the belt. In that regard, she earned a black belt in determination.

We helped the other young woman who was wheelchair-bound develop and adapt self-defense tactics and strategies that gave her a very good chance of thwarting all but the most determined assailant. She was downright scary in her execution and determination; another success.

We also had a blind student who learned to execute the kata and apply self-defense techniques against anyone who dared to lay a hand on her. These three women were a portrait in success and perseverance. They allowed nothing to become an obstacle to achieving progress in martial arts. While they realized that the goal of black belt was not a realistic possibility, they were martial artists just the same, with every bit as much spirit and character as any other. Frankly, teaching them was a humbling experience.

You must consider that what you gain and the character that you develop from overcoming setbacks along the way to your goal is actually more valuable than obtaining the goal itself. Do not lose sight of your goal. There are many small victories you can achieve along the way. Celebrate them. Look at setbacks as opportunities for victories not defeats. Those are the real accomplishments.

* * *

Before we founded United Karate, my wife and other instructors were at a different martial arts school. We attended a black belt test where four of the candidates who were testing for their novice black belts were children. All four were age ten. They had been training several years to reach advanced brown belt. Unfortunately, there were not prepared for their novice black belt test and the instructor who pre-tested them should never have let them pass their pre-test.

Nonetheless, they were all deemed ready for their novice black belt test. The day of the test came and after the adults had been tested on their kata, technical kicks, self-defense and knowledge questions, it was time for the children. The group of four came up and formed a line in front of the panel of judges. They were given the commands and put through their paces to demonstrate their curriculum. They were tested and quizzed on a variety of knowledge questions that all black belt candidates were required to know.

When the testing was completed, the chief instructors and the master of the school did not pass the four young candidates. They were told they could come back in six months and test again. Immediately after the test ended, the parents of two of the children were outraged. They expected their children to pass and literally assumed that paying of the testing fee and passing the pre-test virtually guaranteed passing; not so.

Those parents and their children left the school and their children never continued in martial arts. What a negative, defeatist attitude these parents instilled in their children. What do you think will happen the next time those children attempt something difficult or challenging and do not succeed the first time? It's probably a safe bet that they will simply give up and try something else. Enough of those kinds of experiences and they will learn that maybe they should not try to achieve any goals that might not work out perfectly the first time, so why bother at all?

The other two students met afterward with their parents. They were understandably surprised and disappointed after having passed their pre-test, but the beautiful part of this story is that those other two students showed true martial arts spirit. They were encouraged by their parents and for the next six months, they applied themselves diligently to learning what they had done wrong on the test and what they must do to improve.

They changed the way they practiced, prepared, and trained. They focused intently on their goal. They became more determined than ever. However, what they were determined about was not so much earning their black belt, but changing their ways. In that one instant, when they learned that they had failed their test, they did not see that as a failure as had the other children. These two young warriors saw that they had not prepared appropriately and realized that they needed to change their training routine.

The six months passed quickly. I watched the two students apply themselves in a serious, dedicated manner that an adult would be proud to exhibit. When the day of the test came, their techniques were a joy to watch. Their demonstration of the required knowledge portions of the test was impeccable. Their attitudes were upbeat, enthusiastic, determined and confident. They passed with outstanding scores.

A year later, they went on and passed their test for first-degree black belts in the same manner. They became student instructors helping the adult instructors, assisting, and teaching other children. They entered many tournaments, did very well, and excelled in school. They were successful, not because they earned a black belt, but because they improved their character and attitude. This change led to a long string of successful outcomes in every aspect of their life.

* * *

Nearly the same thing happened to Chuck Norris. In his book, *The Secret of Inner Strength,* he recounts the story of how he failed his first black belt exam. He blanked out completely when it was his turn to demonstrate his techniques and skills. After failing the test, he trained even more seriously and prepared himself. He returned some time later, tested again and passed with high scores. He later went on to become a six-time world champion and achieve great success because he had programmed himself properly to succeed. He did not allow himself to be satisfied with any other outcome. The rest, as they say, is history.

* * *

This is what martial arts is about. This is what success is about. These various students I have spoken about all learned an important lesson about success that impacted the rest of their lives, unfortunately so did the two students who failed their black belt test. You can choose success or you can choose failure. The choice is always yours. Choose wisely.

The Journey is the Reward

The real accomplishment of the two junior giants in the previous section was the acknowledgement that to achieve a desired goal required a change; a change that may not be easy or come quickly. The students learned that they had to change course and embark upon their journey in the right way. You could say that two of the students allowed the dark side of the force to take over, while the other two embraced the light side of the force; positive Chi vs. negative Chi. The positive direction always requires more effort; the negative approach comes very easily.

It has been said many times in many motivational books that success is a journey not a destination and that the journey is the reward. It is true. Martial arts study is a lifetime process of improvement and development. As I have said, the quest to become an excellent martial artist requires you to develop body, mind and spirit. Part of this process of development is to stop, reflect, and appreciate your progress.

There is a famous quote from Master Gichin Funakoshi the founder of Shotokan Karate, "The goal of martial arts is the perfection of the individual's character." If you stray from this pursuit, then you have left the path of the martial artist and you are nothing more than a fighter or a failure. Reflect often on your progress and goals. You should always set new goals for the future that build on your previous accomplishments, but occasionally look back and reflect on the past.

You will see that developing physical skills is relatively routine and straightforward. You will see that learning strategies and how to apply these physical skills in combat or competition takes a little more effort. You will also see that developing and maintaining the spirit and character of a martial artist and an attitude of success is a lifelong endeavor and requires the most significant change. It is an endless journey with endless reward. Reflect more on the spirit of martial arts and the elements of success than on skill or strategy. Do this often and keep a good spirit about you because of all of the qualities of a martial artist, those that define your character are the most important.

As you become a martial artist, you are actually becoming yourself, more than you ever would be if you had chosen another path; you are becoming the you that has been inside waiting to be realized. You are defining and refining yourself. No other sport or physical activity has so many character building qualities as martial arts. The great masters through the ages believed that studying lethal arts helped develop character and that development of character was an essential aspect of studying martial arts. It is a curious thing that you may understand first on the surface of it, but you will only feel it deeply and know it when you have become a martial artist with good spirit and a balance of skill, strategy and character to help you achieve success in martial arts or in anything.

The confidence and character that you develop in martial arts helps you become the you that has always been possible. If you had not undertaken this course, many personal, potential qualities would have been left undeveloped, never to be realized. Although the ultimate purpose of martial skill is to develop the ability to defend or kill, you are developing the skills, character and spirit to live, protect and serve.

As you reflect upon what you are learning and feeling, you will eventually discover that as you master the skills that can kill a man, you are unknowingly developing the skills to let him live and not feel threatened by him. You cannot ever know how much further you have to go, but through reflection, you can at least see how far you have come on this journey and that is your reward.

Seventeen Techniques for Success

"Today will come and go. It can be filled with actions that take you closer to success or further from your dreams. Choose actions that will take you to your dreams."

   Kevin Brett

1. Dream big
Do not limit your dreams or vision of success. Keep it focused on what you really want. Find your purpose or your vision. If you don't have a dream or vision that's ok. You can borrow someone else's. You can follow a path that has been taken by someone else whom you admire or aspire to be like. Eventually you will discover or refine your own goals and dreams and make them more your own.

2. Write down your dream
Describe it. Why do you want this? How will it make you happy? Make it as real as you can so that you will be able to visualize it easily. Write it down in detail and don't leave anything out.

3. Identify the gaps
What building blocks do you need to accomplish this dream? What are the pre-requisites; and what are their pre-requisites. Map out your shopping list of stuff you have to do to get there. Identify the general objectives, then break down the first objective into a detailed "punch list" of actions you need to accomplish. Then start checking off those smaller activities to accomplish each larger objective.

Gaps also apply to gaps in your knowledge or skill. You will need to sit down and take some time to do some soul searching. Write down your strengths and weaknesses; your likes and dislikes; skills and talents. Be honest with yourself. Once you have made these lists, go to some friends who know you well and ask them for their honest opinion about your strengths and weaknesses. This will help you determine where to concentrate part of your efforts and where to seek help.

When you accomplish a certain objective then revisit your list and timeline of objectives. Look at how they are prioritized and review them to see if any adjustments need to be made. Often you will probably not change the objectives or goals, but maybe the way in which you will accomplish them will change. Use creative solutions and approaches.

4. Set goals and prioritize activities
A dream or lofty goal requires many stepping-stones to achieve. You cannot eat the entire elephant in one bite. You must breakdown your ultimate objective into smaller manageable activities and pursue them. This requires planning and organization. Just start making a list of what steps it will take to get you to where you want to be. What resources, knowledge and skills will you need? Get organized. Track your progress and adjust your goals slightly as needed to ensure that these are the right goals to lead you to your dream.

5. Make sacrifices
Adjust to your new reality. You will have to change; who you are, what you do, what you think, who you know and how you live. Change is essential and unavoidable if you are to accomplish anything worthwhile.

6. Start now
You're burning daylight, as John Wayne would say. Be efficient and stay focused only on those activities that will bring you closer to the finish line. Do not become sidetracked by little things that can distract your time, energy and focus. Do not over analyze your plan. Do not spend too much time trying to develop the perfect

plans. The biggest problem that people have when they make plans is that they fail to execute them and actually put them into action. They keep refining their plans thinking that if they have the perfect plan it will get them to their goals faster. Not true. The sooner you start with a reasonable idea of where you are going, the sooner you can make course adjustments on your way to actually getting there!

7. Change your daily routine
If you want to achieve success and become excellent at something or reach a goal you have set then you must change your daily habits and activities. You must begin to include those activities that will help you complete something that brings you closer to your dream. If you do not change yourself, then change will not come to your life.

8. Get plenty of rest
You're going to need it. If you are not well rested, you will not think straight. You will not last throughout the day and have the energy to put in the effort needed on your goals and you will become sick more easily and more often.

9. Get plenty of exercise
Stay healthy so you have the energy and physical ability to accomplish any goal. Exercise will make you feel better by releasing hormones into your bloodstream that will improve your attitude and outlook. You will feel better so that you can enjoy your successes more!

10. Get organized
Know what you need to do each day toward your goals. Review your punch list. Organize any notes, materials, supplies or other items you will need each day. Make sure you have all of your contacts organized; your notes on your progress and next steps so that you will not waste valuable time rummaging through junk.

11. Get up 30 minutes earlier
This will give you extra time to review actions for that day; review your dream statement; read some words of encouragement in a

favorite inspirational book; review a few favorite quotes you have pasted to your bathroom mirror or refrigerator or just spend a few minutes stretching and doing some light exercise to get revved up for the day.

12. Make progress every day
Be persistent and determined. You cannot become a black belt by working out once per week or attending class once per week. You will have to find a way to work three or more classes or workouts into your weekly schedule. If you do not give priority to your goals, they will never be accomplished. You must make a commitment to your goals. Always remember that progress is continuous improvement not just a flash in the pan. You cannot have a three-hour workout on one day per week and think that will have the same effect as working out for one hour, three times per week. Continuous incremental effort is what helps you. You must be in it for the long haul. If you are trying to lose weight as you always hear people say, it requires a lifestyle change. You cannot watch what you eat for a week and then spend the next several weeks breaking all the rules and expect to lose any weight. Even if you have lost a few pounds in the beginning, a long, sustained change in your eating and exercise habits is the only surefire way to lose weight. Anything else is simply an aid to facilitate the process.

13. Be excellent every day
You cannot simply make progress every day. That is not the whole story. You must be excellent every day. In everything you do, no matter how mundane, find some small way to improve upon it; to make it excellent; better than before. Pay attention to details. This is all part of achieving success and excellence. You can't just be good some of the time. You need to develop a mindset of excellence that becomes the way you live, work, play and relate to others. Be careful; do not confuse excellence with perfection. Perfection is a pursuit that can actually take you off course from your goals because perfection in everything is not generally possible and the time required to do or make something perfect can keep you from your bigger goals. Excellent is far above outstanding or even great. Excellent effort and progress will get you there.

14. Hang around successful people and success-minded people

You will need a network of people who support you, encourage you and can share in your dream with you. Hanging around people who are discouraging and pessimistic will only drag you down and provide negative mental programming. A real friend will not discourage you or make you despair. That should give you some clues. Frankly, that would be subjecting yourself to a form of emotional abuse. We all need encouragement and support from time to time and people who are used to achieving goals like you will likely know other people who can help you achieve your goals or provide inspiration. Hanging around successful people will help you pick up successful habits. You will have role models and confidants from whom you can learn.

15. Get inspired

Find your inspiration and revisit it often. Your dream is your main inspiration. Your goals that lead to that dream are your secondary inspiration. Quotes, books, people, music, visual aids (pictures of your goal) and other devices can help give you the encouraging mental boost you will likely need from time to time to help pull you through any difficulties and challenges. These devices of inspiration, whether it is a picture of a particular inspirational person whom you admire, a picture of your actual goal, or a favorite quote posted somewhere are like your daily vitamins. You'll need to take your daily supplement or it is easy to lose track of your goal when you get bogged down into the details.

16. Become a people person

Whatever your goals, you will not be able to accomplish them alone. You will need a coach, confidant, mentor, advisors, critics, supporters, friends, subject-matter experts and so on. You will need to be comfortable meeting and getting to know new people. You must meet many people and keep their contacts. Ask them questions about what they do; what successes they have experienced; what goals or visions are they working on now; share your goals or dreams with them and ask them how they would approach them and then listen.

17. Never, never, never give up

I was at Boy Scout camp with my son this summer and we were having lunch in the mess hall. An old retired Marine Corps Major who was the Chief of Staff of the camp stepped up on the speaking platform. It was his turn to provide a history lesson for the day. He encouraged the boys to work hard on their requirements and merit badges and reminded them that each of them had the potential to earn Eagle Scout. Then he told a story about a U.S. Naval Academy graduation one year when Sir Winston Churchill had been invited as the guest of honor.

Sir Churchill had been asked to speak at the graduation. The midshipmen and the audience were excited and waited with anticipation to hear what words of wisdom the great man brought with him from across the ocean. When it was time, Sir Churchill made his way to the podium. He looked over the crowd, waited a moment and spoke these words, "Gentlemen, never, never, never give up." Then he left.

Achieving black belt, completing a college degree, losing twenty or more pounds, developing the ability to run a marathon, becoming a successful businessperson, having successful relationships and a close-knit family will require you to learn and implement virtually every one of the character qualities described in this book. It may seem a bit daunting at first, but remember you will gradually improve in various ways on various days and success will not come overnight.

The Five Elements of Success

This section covers a basic template or pattern of success. Any dream or vision that you intend to accomplish has to be written down and then broken up into discrete tasks. It's true, success begins with a vision, but it takes more than just a dream. It's the work behind the scenes that will make the dream into a reality.

Great goals cannot be accomplished entirely alone. You will need friends, relatives, mentors, coaches and others who can form a support network to encourage, advice, motivate you, and hopefully provide objective feedback on your progress, potential and direction. Most important you must want your goal – badly. You must want it enough to change your life to accomplish your goals. Success is a mindset, which leads to a life-style.

Below are the basics of planning for success. Read each of the steps below, document everything mentioned and build yourself a plan for your future. Review it with your most trusted advisors and confidants to get their input.

1, Vision: Your Dream
- After writing down your dream, vision, or goal, describe it in detail. Write until you can clearly envision it.
- What types of people (professions, occupations, talents, expertise) will I need to help me?
- Why do I want to do this? How badly do I want it?
- Is it bigger than me or how can I make it about more than just me? Who else might benefit from my success?

2. General Resources and Requirements
- What personal or organizational capabilities will I need to accomplish this goal?
- What personal or organizational resources will I need?
- What knowledge areas or skills will I need to improve or develop?
- What general strengths do I have to help in this quest?
- How can I capitalize on them and leverage my strengths?
- What are my biggest weaknesses that may hold me up or slow me down?
- How can I improve myself to overcome these?

3. Changes
- How will I change my daily routine? Additions/deletions
- What will be my sources of inspiration? Books, quotes, pictures, music, people, movies.

4. Goals and Objectives
- Where do I start?
- What are the top three to seven goals?

5. Goal-Specific Resources and Requirements
- What resources and capabilities do I need to accomplish each specific goal?
- Who can help with a given goal?
- What steps do I need to accomplish each of the goals or objectives?

Review your goals and progress often. Make sure you have the support and resources you need to continue each step of the way. And remember, success is not a destination it is a journey and a way of life that can make the way you live life more rewarding and fulfilling. If you change yourself and your habits, your life will change – deep isn't it? I warned you about that Yoda thing.

Success is finding your purpose and pursuing something that you really enjoy. To find your purpose you must think about what you really enjoy and what you love to do. If you pursue something that you truly love, then you will be successful and you will have no trouble staying motivated. How many successful people have achieved a lot by doing something they do not enjoy? Find your passion and you will find the seed of your success.

The Secret of the Martial Arts

There is no single, universal secret to success in martial arts. There is no formula for greatness. The secrets to success lie inside each individual.

A thousand martial artists can have a thousand different kinds of success. You cannot have the success of these thousand however; you can only have the success that is yours. You have achieved it for yourself. Do not be afraid that others will take your success because the success is you and your unique journey. It is what you have made of yourself. Success only has meaning because of you and what you bring to it and how it has changed you.

The balance between the physical skill of your body, the mental strategies in your mind and the spiritual development of your character is the true secret to martial arts that is yours to discover.

* * *

This is not the end of the book. If this were really the end of the book it would mean that everything worth saying about these topics has been covered in these few pages. As you begin or continue your journey as a martial artist and as a warrior, you will see that this is not possible. This is not the end of the book, but simply the place where I chose to leave off. This is the point at which you must engage in your own martial quest. This is the point at which you must begin or continue your journey and discover your own secrets ... they are waiting.

Find your passion.
Begin your journey.
Serve a purpose bigger than yourself.
Pursue your vision.
Realize your dream.
Have fun.
Good luck!

The Beginning

Appendix A

Framework for Martial Arts Study

The following is a suggested framework for martial arts study. It does not discuss specific techniques of a given style of martial arts, but categories of techniques, skills, training and knowledge for a well-rounded martial arts course of study. The framework is broken into blocks of material that form discrete levels or belts in the classical sense of rank advancement. In each level, there are opportunities to refer back to this book and review related passages for additional study, development and consideration. The intent here was to take the topics covered and referenced throughout this book and put them into a cohesive framework to guide your studies and growth. Enjoy!

Framework for Martial Arts Study	
Beginner: Level 1	
Self-Defense Techniques	Defenses against: • Side headlock • Rear bear hug with arms free • Front grab • Rear arm lock & grab • Two-handed arm grab • Two-handed low push • Hook punch • Wrist grab • Rear bear hug with arms pinned • Two-handed push • Reverse punch
Review related passages in "The Way of the Martial Artist"	
Fighting Skills	• Simple chokes and holds (escapes) • Kicks • Punches • Hand strikes

	• Elbow strikes • Basic movement and footwork • Basic throws and takedowns • Blocks and deflection: deflecting hand techniques • Joint manipulation (wrist, elbow) • Basic weapons of opportunity

Physical Conditioning Skills	• Flexibility:
	   o Stretches
	   o Joint mobility
	• Strength
	• Stamina
	• Speed
	• Timing
	• Coordination
	• Balance: Basic static posture and balance points

Mental Skills	• Weapons of the body
	   o Hands, feet, elbow, arm, fingers
	   o Knee, leg, foot
	• Targets of the body: centerline – front and back
	• Relaxation
	• Meditation – clearing the mind focusing on nothing to prepare a training session
	• Minor training injuries
	• Beginning first aid
	• Martial arts history: origins of your style
	• Wilderness survival: basics (shelter, water, fire, winter weather techniques, basic signaling)
	• Basic Anatomy (skeletal system)

Character	• Marital Ethics:
	   o The Line of Conviction
	   o The Force Continuum

Framework for Martial Arts Study	
Beginner: Level 2	
Self-Defense Techniques	Defenses against: • Forearm grab • One-handed lapel grab • One-handed push • Head lock and punch • Ground attack • Two-hand wrist grab • Cross arm push
Review related passages in "The Way of the Martial Artist"	
Fighting Skills	• Chokes and holds (escapes) • Kicks • Hand strikes: knife hands • More movement and footwork • Deflection: deflecting kicks • Joint manipulation (wrist, elbow) • Basic ground fighting

Physical Conditioning Skills	• Flexibility:
	   o More stretches
	   o Joint mobility
	• Strength
	• Stamina
	• Speed
	• Timing
	• Coordination
	• Balance: Basic posture while executing hand strikes and blocks

Mental Skills	• Meditation – focusing the mind on visualization of techniques to improve technique development • Beginning first aid • Martial arts history: Types and uses of classical weapons • Wilderness survival: basics – additional techniques (shelter, water, fire, winter weather techniques, additional signaling techniques) • Basic Anatomy (circulatory system)
Character	• Respect, Emotion, Revenge, Attitude

Framework for Martial Arts Study	
Intermediate: Level 3	
Self-Defense Techniques	Defenses against: • Two-handed choke hold • Two-handed rear choke • Cross wrist grab • Two-handed wrist grab from behind • Back leg front kick • Ground attack • Front hair grab • Front tackle
Review related passages in "The Way of the Martial Artist"	
Fighting Skills	• Chokes and holds (escaping) • Sweeps and takedowns (executing) • Basic vital point strikes (front centerline) • Beginning free-style sparing • Deflecting blows from clubs • Basic ground fighting
Physical Conditioning Skills	• Flexibility: More stretches • Strength • Stamina • Speed • Timing • Coordination • Balance: Posture in sparring
Mental Skills	• Meditation – focusing the mind on visualization of scenarios to improve situational awareness • First aid • Martial arts history: Survey of various Chinese and Japanese styles • Medical implications of martial techniques (related to basic vital point strikes) • Wilderness survival: basics – additional techniques (shelter, water, fire, food, hot weather techniques, basic land navigation) • Basic Anatomy (nervous system)
Character	• Ego, Self-Reliance, Confidence, Self-Confidence

Framework for Martial Arts Study	
Intermediate: Level 4	
Self-Defense Techniques	Defenses against: • Back leg round kick • Full nelson • Hair grab from behind • Ground attack • Step-behind sidekick • Rear arm lock with collar grab • One-hand back push
Review related passages in "The Way of the Martial Artist"	
Fighting Skills	• Chokes and holds (escaping) • Sweeps and takedowns (detecting and countering) • Avoiding & escape multiple opponents • Basic vital point strikes (back centerline) • Deflecting knife and bladed weapon strikes
Physical Conditioning Skills	• Vision and perception: sight, observations, detection • Coordination • Realism training: outdoor training modes: diverse weather
Mental Skills	• Martial arts history: Survey of weapon styles • Medical implications of martial techniques (related to basic vital point strikes) • Wilderness survival: intermediate – additional techniques (shelter, water, fire, food, hot weather techniques, land navigation)
Character	• Humility, Conviction, Reflection

Framework for Martial Arts Study	
Intermediate: Level 5	
Self-Defense Techniques	Defense against: • Back kick • Double rear arm lock • Arm grab • Two-arm back push
Review related passages in "The Way of the Martial Artist"	
Fighting Skills	• Chokes and holds (applying) • Avoiding & escaping multiple opponents • Basic vital point strikes (back centerline) • Weapons of opportunity: using your environment (indoors: office, bus, train, plane, home) • Classical weapon of choice • Basic firearm takeaways • Joint manipulation (ankle, leg locks)
Physical Conditioning Skills	• Coordination • Realism training: outdoor training modes: diverse terrain
Mental Skills	• Martial arts history: Survey of warrior societies: Samurai and European knights • Medical implications of martial techniques (related to basic vital point strikes) • Wilderness survival: intermediate – additional techniques (food, terrain-specific techniques: woodlands)
Character	• Honor

Framework for Martial Arts Study	
Intermediate: Level 6	
Self-Defense Techniques	Defenses against: • Front snap kick • Rear choke with arm lock • Two-handed front choke • Grab and sweep kick • Multiple attackers • Two-handed grab • Push or punch • Multiple attackers
Review related passages in "The Way of the Martial Artist"	
Fighting Skills	• Chokes and holds (applying) • Avoiding & escaping multiple opponents • Joint manipulation (ankle, leg locks) • Throws and falls • Weapons of opportunity: using your environment (outdoors: branches, rocks, sand, outdoor implements) • Classical weapon of choice • Firearm takeaways • Basic knife fighting techniques
Physical Conditioning Skills	• Coordination • Realism training: outdoor training modes: blindfolded or at night
Mental Skills	• Martial arts history: Survey of warrior societies: Native American warrior tribes • Wilderness survival: intermediate – additional techniques (food, terrain-specific techniques: dessert/barren terrain)
Character	• Chi

Framework for Martial Arts Study	
Advanced: Level 7	
Self-Defense Techniques	• Escape from a gang of several assailants • Defense against multiple assailants with weapons • Camouflage, concealment and evasion techniques
Review related passages in "The Way of the Martial Artist"	
Fighting Skills	• Ground fighting • Pressure points • Modern firearm use • Knife fighting techniques
Physical Conditioning Skills	• Realism training: Gang attacks, parking lot scenarios, sub-way/train/bus scenarios • Camouflage, concealment and evasion – surviving intruders or avoiding captors
Mental Skills	• Martial arts history: Survey of ancient warriors - Spartans • Medical implications of martial techniques (related to basic vital point strikes)
Character	• Spirit and Excellence

Appendix B

A Quote for Success and Motivation for Each Week of the Year

1. "Why talk about the future if you're not going to build it." – Walt Disney

2. "One person with a belief is equal to a force of 99 who have only interests." – John Stuart Mill

3. "If you think you can't you're right. If you think you can, you're right." – Henry Ford

4. "A professional is someone who can do his best work when he doesn't feel like it." – Alistair Cooke

5. "Success or failure is caused more by mental attitude than by mental capacity." – Sir Walter Scott

6. "The secret of success in life is for a man to be ready for his opportunity when it comes." – Benjamin Disraeli

7. "All virtue lies in individual action, in inward energy, in self-determination. There is no moral worth in being swept away by a crowd even toward the best objective." – William Channing

8. "The future is now." – George Allen (Former Head Coach, Washington Redskins)

9. "Nothing in the world can take the place of persistence. Talent will not; nothing is more common than unsuccessful men with talent. Genius will not; the world is full of educated derelicts. Persistence and determination alone are omnipotent. The

slogan 'press on' has solved and always will solve the problems of the human race." – Calvin Coolidge

10. "There's no such thing as a self-made man. I've had much help and have found that if you are willing to work; many people are willing to help you." - O. Wayne Rollins

11. "Success seems to be largely a matter of hanging on after others have let go." – William Feather

12. "Keep away from people who try to belittle your ambition. Small people always do that, but the really great make you feel that you too, can become great." – Mark Twain

13. "Never, never, never give up." – Sir Winston Churchill

14. "Every great man, every successful man, no matter what the field of endeavor, has known the magic that lies in these words: Every adversity has the seed of an equivalent or greater benefit." – W. Clement Stone

15. "Inch by inch, anything's a cinch." – Dr. Robert Schuller

16. "Don't let the opinions of the average man sway you. Dream and he thinks you're crazy. Succeed, and he thinks you're lucky. Acquire wealth, and he thinks you're greedy. Pay no attention. He simply doesn't understand." – Robert G. Allen

17. "Someday I hope to enjoy enough of what the world calls success so that someone will ask me, 'What's the secret of it?' I shall say simply this: 'I get up when I fall down.'" – Paul Harvey

18. "It is not the critic who counts; not the man who points out how the strong man stumbled, or where the doer of deeds could have done them better. The credit belongs to the man who is actually in the arena, whose face is marred by dust and sweat and blood; who strives valiantly; who errs and comes short again and again; who knows the great enthusiasms, the great

devotions; who spends himself in a worthy cause; who at the best, knows in the end the triumph of high achievement, and who, at the worst, if he fails, at least fails while daring greatly, so that his place shall never be with those timid souls who know neither victory nor defeat." – Theodore Roosevelt

19. "History records the successes of men with objectives and a sense of direction. Oblivion is the position of small men overwhelmed by obstacles." – William H. Danforth

20. "Industry, thrift, and self-control are not sought because they create wealth, but because they create character." – Calvin Coolidge

21. "Progress always involves risk. You can't steal second base and keep your foot on first." – Frederick B. Wilcox

22. "Ultimately we know deeply that the other side of every fear is a freedom." – Marilyn Ferguson

23. "One man with courage makes a majority." – Andrew Jackson

24. "The life which is unexamined is not worth living." – Plato

25. "The more you do of what you've done, the more you'll have of what you've got." - Anonymous

26. "The winners in life think constantly in terms of, I can, I will and I am. Losers, on the other hand, concentrate their waking thoughts on what they should have or would have done, or what they can't do." – Dr. Dennis Waitley

27. "To know and not to do is not yet to know." – Zen saying

28. "Wealth is when small efforts produce big results. Poverty is when big efforts produce small results." – George David, M.D.

29. "Luck is a word used to describe the success of people you don't like." – Charles Jarvis

30. "Practice all of your scales. Learn to play the blues in every key. Practice all of your arpeggios and etudes, and then forget all of that stuff and just play!" – Charlie "Bird" Parker (Jazz Saxophonist)

31. "Success is not something that can be measured or worn on a watch or hung on the wall. It is not the esteem of colleagues, or the admiration of the community, or the appreciation of patients. Success is the certain knowledge that you have become yourself, the person you were meant to be from all time. That should be reward enough." – Dr. George Sheehan

32. "The man who does not work for the love of work, but only for money is not likely to make money or to find much fun in life." – Charles M. Schwab

33. "I would rather see a crooked furrow than a field unplowed." – Paul Jewkes

34. "My life seems to be one long obstacle course, with me as the chief obstacle." – Jack Paar

35. "Don't compete. Create. Find out what everyone else is doing and then don't do it." – Joel Weldon

36. "I shall be telling this with a sigh, somewhere ages and ages hence: Two roads diverged in a wood, and I took the one less traveled by and that has made all the difference." – Robert Frost

37. "Goals are as essential to success as air is to life." – David Schwartz

38. "There is no security on this earth; there is only opportunity." – Douglas MacArthur

39. "Some men have thousands of reasons why they cannot do what they want to, when all they need is one reason why they can." – Dr. Willis R. Whitney

40. "No man is free who is not master of himself." – Epictetus

41. "We know too much and are convinced of too little." – T.S. Eliot

42. "You can get everything in life that you want if you'll just help enough other people get what they want." – Zig Ziglar

43. "If I had eight hours to chop down a tree, I'd spend six sharpening my ax." – Abraham Lincoln

44. "Successful people make decisions quickly (as soon as all the facts are available) and change them very slowly (if ever). Unsuccessful people make decisions very slowly, and change them often and quickly." – Napoleon Hill

45. "Talk does not cook rice." – Chinese Proverb

46. "Unjust criticism is usually a disguised compliment. It often means you have aroused jealousy and envy. Remember that no one ever kicks a dead dog." – Dale Carnegie

47. If you can imagine it, you can achieve it; if you can dream it, you can become it." – William Arthur Ward

48. "Motivation is what gets you started. Habit is what keeps you going." – Jim Ryun

49. "Obstacles are things that a person sees when he takes his eyes off his goals." – E. Joseph Cossman

50. "The most practical, beautiful, workable philosophy in the world won't work – if you don't" – Zig Ziglar

51. "Choice, not circumstance determines your success." - Anonymous

52. "Success is not the key to happiness. Happiness is the key to success. If you love what you are doing, you will be successful." – Dr. Albert Schweitzer

About the Author

Kevin Brett is the President and CEO of Kevin Brett Studios, Incorporated of Stafford, Virginia. He is a certified martial arts instructor with twenty years of martial arts training and teaching experience. Kevin is an experienced outdoorsman and survival practitioner.

He and his wife Lana Kaye Brett were two of the five co-founders of the United Karate Institute of Self-Defense, Incorporated in Alexandria, Virginia. He has taught martial arts and self-defense combat classes to local law enforcement, military and federal agents focusing on realistic and practical application of martial arts techniques.

Kevin developed martial arts curriculum, programs and training material for all belt ranks at United Karate. He has developed comprehensive student manuals and more than a dozen videos for all of the United Karate belt levels. He has competed in martial arts at the local and national level and has studied and cross-trained extensively in Tae Kwon Do, Shotokan, American Kenpo Karate, Sambo, Jiu-Jitsu, Kenjutsu and Tai Chi.

For more information and to see other books and videos from Kevin Brett Studios, Incorporated visit us on the web:

Kevin Brett
S T U D I O S

Entertainment | Education | Family

www.KevinBrettStudios.com

Acknowledgements

Photographic and artistic credits:

Alexandra Brett
p. 11

Kevin Brett
p. 12,17,37,48

Wikipedia – public domain – Wikimedia Commons
p. 13,22

William Brett
p.29,33,39,41,45,50,52,54,57,58,60,61,62,64,65,66,67,68,69,72,74,77, 80,81,82,85,86,87,88,89,90,91,92,94,95,96,104,105,122,124,125,126, 130,139,141

U.S. Department of Defense – public domain
p. 21,73,143,144

Index

A

Adaptability, 28
Appearances, 137
Appreciation, 164
Attacking, 134
Attitude, 152
Awareness, 46

B

Balance, 35
Breathing, 39
Bushido, 17, 18

C

Change, 43, 196, 197
Character, 147
Chi, 13, 24, 42, 43, 44, 45, 148,
    149, 150, 151, 166, 176, 183,
    186, 193, 211, 219
Conviction, 159, 206
Coordinated, 31
Coordination, 31
Creativity, 128, 142

D

Deception, 128
Decisiveness, 126
Dim Mak, 75
Disney, 5, 182
Distance, 34
Distraction, 127, 129
Dream, 201

E

Ego, 154
Energy, 46
Enlightenment, 170
Etiquette, 153
Excellence, 147
Experimentation, 132

F

Fakes, 127
First aid, 208
Focus, 42
Footwork, 38

G

Ground fighting, 212

H

Happiness, 1, 161
Healing, 99
Honor, 172
Humility, 159
Hyper flexion, 79

I

Innovative, 132, 155
Integrity, 158

K

Kicking, 61

M

Marine Corps, 20, 73, 144, 200
MCMAP, 20, 21
Meditation, 42
Movement, 37

O

Okinawa, 87
Opposites, 117, 129

P

Passion, 175
Perception, 51
Posture, 36
Practice, 96
Punching, 63

Q

Qualities, 7

R

Reaction, 34
Realism, 30
Recycle, 123
Relax, 40, 41, 42, 206
Respect, 153
Revenge, 152
Rhythm, 59

S

Self-Confidence, 158
Self-Defense, 121
Self-Reliance, 156
Strategy, 138, 140
Stretching, 98
Success, 185, 195, 200
Survival, 6, 105

T

Tactics, 115
Tea Ceremony, 18
Teaching, 109
Theory, 116
Thought, 47, 120
Timing, 32, 206, 207, 208
Training, vii, 27, 30, 46, 105

U

Understanding, 51

V

Versatility, 29
Vulnerabilities, 125

W

Walt Disney, 5, 182
Warrior, 164
Weapons, 76, 123

Z

Zanshin, 160
Zen, 169

www.ingramcontent.com/pod-product-compliance
Lightning Source LLC
Chambersburg PA
CBHW070952040426

42443CB00007B/476